night vision

night vision

seeing ourselves
through dark moods

mariana alessandri

PRINCETON UNIVERSITY PRESS

PRINCETON AND OXFORD

Published by Princeton University Press
41 William Street, Princeton, New Jersey 08540
99 Banbury Road, Oxford OX2 6JX

press.princeton.edu

All Rights Reserved
ISBN 9780691215457
ISBN (e-book) 9780691242682

British Library Cataloging-in-Publication Data is available

Editorial: Rob Tempio and Chloe Coy
Production Editorial: Sara Lerner
Text and Jacket Design: Karl Spurzem
Production: Erin Suydam
Publicity: Maria Whelan and Carmen Jimenez
Copyeditor: Cynthia Buck

Epigraph Credit: From Gloria Anzaldúa, *Borderlands/La Frontera: The New Mestiza*. San Francisco: Aunt Lute Books, 2012, 60.

This book has been composed in Arno Pro

Printed on acid-free paper. ∞

Printed in the United States of America

10 9 8 7 6 5 4 3 2 1

To everyone who is, in Dr. Gloria Anzaldúa's words,
"excruciatingly alive to the world," especially my students

contents

night vision

introduction

doubting the light

There are times, many of which we keep secret, when we free-fall into darkness—long days of obscurity and shadow, hours of doubt that cloud the mind, depression so deep it seems impossible to see a way forward. All we want is a little light, a little clarity, a little sunshine. We long for the dawn of a new day. Even when we're feeling okay, we invoke the light often enough. We "see the light," have a "lightbulb" moment, seek the "light at the end of the tunnel." We're drawn to people who "glow" or have a "radiant" smile. At least in the United States—historically the land of bootstraps, optimism, and the power of positive thinking—we've been raised on a diet of light. We associate it with everything from safety to intelligence to peace to hope to purity to optimism to love to happiness to fun to frivolity. To everything good. Taken together, these little equations make up the Light Metaphor, which holds that bright is preferable to dim, sunshine happier than clouds, and light moods superior to dark moods.

This book is about the urge to pair light with good and dark with bad. We'll explore this pairing's underlying origins, its promises, and, ultimately, its harmful effects. It's understandable that we would want to avoid darkness, but we hurt

1

ourselves chasing the light. What we need going forward is to stop trying to shed light on darkness and instead learn to see in the dark.

Philosophers like me have been thinking about light and dark as metaphors for knowledge and ignorance, good and evil, for almost 2,500 years. Plato suggested this pairing in the *Republic* through the character of Socrates, who tells his friends a story about a group of prisoners forcibly kept in a cave unaware that the sun is just outside. Many philosophers inflict Plato's Allegory of the Cave on defenseless students semester after semester. I do it on the first day of Introduction to Philosophy. As my students* and I read Plato's description of the cave together, I ask them to sketch it on paper. We will interpret its meaning later, I tell them, but since the scene itself is so hard to imagine, we need to get it down on paper first.

"What's in the cave?" I ask.

Prisoners, a wall, fire, some puppeteers, and an exit.

"Position the prisoners first," I say. They're human and we're human, and that seems important. A future philosophy major tells me that the prisoners are chained in three places: neck, wrists, ankles. They are stuck sitting down and cannot turn their heads, even to look around. They see only what's in front of them, but they can hear each other. All day every day the prisoners of Plato's imagination stare at a wall. Poor souls.

"Great. Draw the wall. What's on it?" Out of the corner of my eye I see a quiet freshman doodling, but I suspect she is not drawing the cave. She looks checked out, and she's not the only one.

"Shadows," someone in sweats mumbles.

* All student names have been changed because they represent composite characters.

"Of what?" I push.

"Animals, trees, people." It's common for students to answer this question laconically on the first day of class. They dare not deviate from the script they have been reading from since they were five. In time they will relax and take more risks thinking out loud.

"How'd the shadows get there?" I continue.

A dutiful student announces that puppets are responsible for the shadows on the wall.

"Huh? What puppets?" I ask.

"There's a campfire burning in the cave," someone responds, "and the puppeteers use that light to project shadows of their puppets onto the wall."

"You mean like in a kid's bedroom, where the light of a lamp is enough to throw shadow-puppets?" I clarify.

"Yup."

"Why are people throwing shadows of puppets onto a cave wall?" I ask this question with the confusion of a first-time reader. I want to pique the students' curiosity and make them question Plato's sanity. What they can't see yet is how quickly we will move from clarification-type questions to questions that will make them feel queasy.

No one can tell me why Plato's puppeteers manipulate the minds of the cave prisoners. But they realize the prisoners are mistaking shadows for objects. Never having seen a real tree, they believe that tree-shadows are trees. The prisoners even have contests to determine rank: Who consistently spots the most trees? Who identifies the tallest one? In this cave, your worth is based on how expertly you traverse a world made entirely of shadows.

By this point, we can imagine the cave: it's a dim place filled with sad sacks who spend their lives approximating reality. The students understand why the prisoners don't rebel: they don't know their reality isn't real. Someone suggests that Plato is calling us prisoners. A second student thinks that we believe the media's lies. A third worries that we're living on autopilot. By now, though, we agree that Plato is telling us something. He thinks we're imprisoned together and have gotten something terribly wrong. But we don't know what it is, or how much of our lives we've spent believing it. Some students close their eyes. Others let out the air they have been holding. They are loosening up and looking around at each other in disbelief. They are perplexed.

The story has a happyish ending: One prisoner gets his chains ripped off before being forcibly dragged out of the cave. His body is thrust into the light of day, where he immediately buries his eyes in his elbow. For weeks, he's unable to recognize anything in the light except what looks familiar, like shadows on the ground and reflections on the lake. He is blind until the sun sets, at which time the trees on the riverbank come into focus.

After a long time, our hero starts acclimating to the light. As his eyes adjust, he can make out real trees. In time, he will accept what my students are considering for the first time: even our bedrock beliefs can be wrong.

A typical interpretation of Plato's cave is the one my students land on: the sun saves. My religious students think the sun is God; the atheists prefer to call it Truth. We can at least agree that it's the sun that allows the freed prisoner to truly see the world. Someone compares acclimating to the sun to education. It's a process of crawling out of ignorance and into truth, out of darkness and into light. However painful the sun may be at first, the students admit, it ultimately saves the prisoner. We can all relate. We too have been taught to walk in the light.

By the time I turned eighteen, I'd already collected a fair share of love and light. I'd spent my summers on a hot towel on

Rockaway Beach in New York City. So by the time I was in college learning the Light Metaphor's philosophical origin, I was ready. I graduated clutching one certainty, the same one my students lunge at with both hands so as to stop spinning: light is necessary to know the truth.

The problem with this setup is that I have always felt emotionally dark. I'm an angry person genetically, and I feel sad most of the time. I think the world is overwhelmingly tragic, with just a few rays of sunshine poking through every now and then. Like Winnie-the-Pooh's pessimistic donkey friend, I have always been an Eeyore at heart.

———

If you're like me, you know it's not easy to be an Eeyore in a world that prefers Tiggers, to be a rain cloud who gets told sunshine is best.* It's hard for those of us with a darker disposition to avoid being pelted by positivity, one perky pebble at a time. TV, Twitter, Instagram, Pinterest, podcasts, self-help books, T-shirts, pillows, bumper stickers, coffee mugs, and billboards all want us to live our best life. In the 1980s it was Bobby McFerrin's song "Don't Worry, Be Happy" and Walmart's big yellow smiley face. Today it's "Let Your Light Shine." Dark moods struggle for sympathy in a world that would like to see them corrected, cured, or converted.

To fit into this sun-drenched world, some of us try to fake it till we make it. We remember that some people have it worse than us (which usually makes us feel guilty on top of achy). We call "First World Problems" on ourselves (and take

---

*How and why Tigger became the symbol of bright-sidedness is a mystery if you read him as a nervous wreck who bounces to self-soothe.

on a bonus feeling: shame). And we read books on how to be happier. Book sales suggest that I am not the only one who has exhausted herself chasing the light.

Rachel Hollis's 2018 best-seller *Girl, Wash Your Face* sold over two million copies because that many of us wanted to believe that we can control our happiness with our attitude. Twelve years earlier, *The Secret* and *The Law of Attraction* became best-sellers for the same reason: we wanted to up our return on investment in positive thinking. These are just modern iterations of the 1952 classic *The Power of Positive Thinking*. When Norman Vincent Peale made his debut, Americans made him a best-selling author. In so doing, we agreed to become the Light Metaphor's foot soldiers, repeating the mantras that declare light to be smarter than dark, happiness hipper than sadness, tranquility trendier than anger, and optimism holier than pessimism. We smiled in the face of adversity, attended workshops on anger management, taught our kids that crying is weak, and tried to chemically erase our anxiety, fear, and sadness. We obeyed the Light Metaphor's three commandments: silence, stifle, and swallow your dark moods.

It worked. We beat the darkness. We successfully wrestled our negative feelings way down deep into the oubliettes of our souls, where they got perfectly lost until they disappeared forever. After vanquishing our darkest moods and screwing on happy faces, we lived happily ever after on cloud nine with nary a worry line in sight.*

Or maybe not.

Why not?

Because Plato was wrong. Or at least readers of Plato have been wrong to conclude from his allegory that truth can only

---

*Cloud nine used to be cloud seven. Even our imaginary goalpost for happiness keeps moving.

be found in the light. We were wrong to believe that the sun alone will save us. Worst of all, we failed to consider the intellectual, physical, and emotional cost of putting the sun so high in the sky.

After Plato, the Light Metaphor really took off. Jesus called himself the light of the world. Copernicus declared that the Earth (and everything else) revolves around the sun. Light became our savior and darkness sank under the weight of its homely attributes. Darkness was denigrated (literally, "blackened") and vilified, taking its place in philosophy, religion, and history as scary, ugly, ignorant, and sinful. "My life feels really dark." "I'm in the dark on this one." "I don't want to go back to that dark place." The Light Metaphor relentlessly insists that darkness is ugly, negative, miserable.

Not surprisingly, the Enlightenment philosophies that emerged long after Plato did not go so well for dark-skinned people, who were "scientifically" proven to be less human and less intelligent than light-skinned people. Within their biased framework, whites could scarcely conceive of Black knowledge or wisdom. After the emancipation of enslaved people in the United States, Black men were portrayed as monstrous rapists who terrorized innocent white women. Black women were cast as their sexually insatiable, sinful counterparts. These stereotypes have been immeasurably damaging, and we are not past them yet. Fair and Lovely skin-lightening cream is still used by dark-skinned women who have been convinced that light is luscious and darkness is deficient. Fawning over a newborn's light skin or blue eyes is customary in Latinx communities like mine; not so for dark skin and brown eyes. And although *Night Vision* is not focused on societal prejudice against dark skin as much as on dark moods, the two ideas grew up together. We will never conquer colorism as long as we equate darkness with deformity and deficiency.

In a world that worships light, darkness is made to carry the weight of a hundred ills, including ignorance, ugliness, unpleasantness, gloominess, painfulness, heaviness, monstrousness, and all-around unhealthiness. Forget dark moods—they never stood a chance.

After reading Plato's cave story, my students have a hard time believing they might have been brought up on shadows. Likewise, in writing this book I've had a hell of a time doubting the unequivocal goodness of light. Who wants to argue against cultivating optimism or a cheerful attitude? What American dares to doubt that we make our own happiness or that a sunny disposition leads to financial gain? Who would not want to bask in the light of an $11 billion self-help industry?

Those of us who have been burned by the Light Metaphor, that's who. Anyone who has been told to look on the bright side would be right to think the person saying that sees our anger, sadness, grief, depression, and anxiety as self-indulgent. Few people who offer this advice want to hear about the dark place we are in, or how we think things will not work out this time. People who swear we "make our own sunshine" tend to be short on empathy. They will most likely assume that we're not trying hard enough.

This is the Brokenness Story, and it plays bad cop to the Light Metaphor's good cop. If the Light Metaphor sings, "Happiness is a choice!," the Brokenness Story barks: "What are you sniveling about now?" We hear the Brokenness Story every time we fail to live in the light, when we just cannot make ourselves feel brighter. It's the voice that calls us weak, ungrateful, self-pitying, and self-indulgent. In the name of strength, it shames those of us who do not smile through our pain (or at least grit our teeth and bear it).

Could it be that all this time we've been trying *too* hard? That we've been trying to bleach something that was never meant to be bright? Maybe darkness is the human condition, and maybe not even Tigger can "be like a proton: always positive." In this case, what gets left in the wake of the self-help authors and positivity gurus who rip us in two with their bare hands and a smile are a bunch of divided souls who feel dark but wish we didn't. Instead of feeling human, the angry among us, the hurt, the grieving, the depressed or anxious, have every reason to feel broken.

Does it help or hurt that most of our dark moods are classified as mental illnesses? The light of Western medicine has not been kind to our darkness. Medical terminology for depression, anxiety, grief, sadness, and anger has made us more, not less, biased against darkness. On top of "scary," "ugly," "ignorant," and "sinful," doctors have painted our darker moods as illnesses, diseases, disorders, pathologies, infirmities, ailments, and maladies. These medical terms make a science of our brokenness, of our definitive departure from wholeness. Under the fluorescent lights of psychiatry, it's as difficult to recognize dignity in our dark moods as it was for the newly freed prisoner to recognize a real tree in the middle of the day. No one I know thinks that crying yourself to sleep on the bathroom floor is dignified. But it is very often diagnosable.

Good psychologists will readily admit that there's no agreed-upon definition of disorder, mental illness, or disease. They don't even agree on whether the five moods discussed in this book—anger, sadness, grief, depression, and anxiety—are best categorized as mental illnesses or if they should be called something else. But despite psychology's stab at humility, it is impossible to miss the anxiety "epidemic" among teens, or the millions of people in the United States who are "afflicted" with depression. The terms we use to name our existential conditions are often hostile or scary, not to mention degrading. We are said to be "battling" mental illness or "succumbing" to it by suicide. Words matter: they pit us against ourselves or put us on our own side. "Brain disease" does not exactly inspire a person to honor their depression; "diagnosis" doesn't rhyme with "dignity." "We're all mentally ill" is not nearly as edifying as "anxiety makes you a full-blooded human being." Judging dark moods by how they look in the light yields a vocabulary that makes dignity hard to spot. Learning to see our painful moods in the dark will involve adopting new words for old woes.

By now the research is clear that pretending to be brighter—turning our frowns upside down—hurts us. We have heard that we can make ourselves sick—literally, emotionally, mentally—by suppressing or avoiding negative feelings. With help from authors like Kate Bowler, Brené Brown, Austin Channing Brown, Tarana Burke, Susan David, Glennon Doyle, and Julie K. Norem, and propelled by movements like Me Too and Black Lives Matter, some of us are experimenting with not drying our eyes or washing our faces. Some of us have begun leaning into the dark side of our emotional spectrum.

To some extent, it's working. Some of us experienced a rush of recognition the first time we heard the term "toxic positivity," because although we had felt the oppressive phenomenon for years, we did not know we could name it. Talking about depression and grief seems more okay since the onset of the Covid-19 pandemic. We have plenty of evidence that we are not alone, and it's nice to see people letting their dark hair down. When billboards tell us that depression is

not laziness, that anxiety is not weakness, and that anger, sadness, and grief are dark moods that everyone struggles with,
it becomes easier to believe that there are more out there like
us. Mental health campaigns like makeitok.org tell us, "You're
not alone."

Still, it's hard not to finish that sentence with, ". . . because
we're *all* broken." "You need not be ashamed of your anxiety
because 30 percent of Americans are in the same boat" may be
closer to the truth than "anxiety is a sin," but it's not as true as
"anxiety means you're paying attention."[1] Shining a spotlight on
anxiety and depression can show us the size of the boat we
share. But it cannot offer us dignity.

Self-help books be damned: you can't build a positive self-
concept on brokenness. You can't draw encouraging conclusions about dark moods by looking at them in the light.

Even the fiercest defender of dark moods—someone who
believes that darkness is more than failed light—still feels
pressure to lighten up. The same person who knows that
#staypositive burns them will let slip words like "pity-party"
or "wallow" to describe their darker moments.

For example, I might defend a woman's right to anger by day
but experience shame in the dead of night if that angry woman
turns out to be me. When we are alone, we may wonder whether
those manifestation folks are right in claiming that we attract
what we put into the world. We might even worry that the all-
the-feels movement will fail us. Vulnerability might just leave
us exposed. Chasing emotional balance has left many of us ambivalent: we agree in principle to stop denying our dark moods
but still feel shame when they overcome us. Even as we gain
emotional intelligence, the Light Metaphor reminds us that,
come midnight, we'll be praying for daylight just as surely as

our neighbor's kitchen reads: "Stay Positive: Better Days Are on Their Way."

When I fall into the hands of the Brokenness Story and begin to wonder if God does sometimes make junk, I take refuge in philosophy. Two millennia after Plato came the Existentialists. This is a group—half of whom reject the term "Existentialist"— who believe that life is really, really hard. They see humans as the ones who hold your hair while you vomit and hold your hand while you die. They believe that we have an intense capacity for sadness, along with unsounded depths of rage and anxiety, grief, and depression. For them it's no mystery: we walk barefoot on this craggy earth and watch our loved ones grow cancer. Existentialists understand why we spend so much time devising ways to avoid thinking dark thoughts. They write about how we lie to ourselves and each other, how we say we're fine when we're not and find excuses not to talk to our kids about death. Existentialists write things like, "Hell is other people," and, "To love is to suffer."[2] For me, it was love at first sight. Existentialists have been helping me see dignity in darkness for over twenty years.

Before medical health professionals and superstar bloggers took over the job of narrating our psychic lives, philosophers were the primary storytellers of the soul (or the *doctors*, if you asked the ancients). The philosophers whose stories I share in this book spent significant time exploring their caves and recounting what they saw there. None of them will object if you wear black and listen to Morrissey—nor will they require it. They will let us think about death and decay without calling us "morbid" or "dramatic." When we need shelter from the light, we can turn to these six Existential philosophers who were intimates of darkness: Audre Lorde, María Lugones, Miguel de

Unamuno, C. S. Lewis, Gloria Anzaldúa, and Søren Kierke-gaard.[3] They can provide shade for us when the sun starts to burn. The words they used and the positions they took on anger, sadness, grief, depression, and anxiety help me hold my head high. I'm hoping they will help you too.

The central questions of this book are: What if truth, goodness, and beauty reside not only in light but also in darkness? What if believing otherwise has been a huge mistake? All this time we have been taught to be biased against darkness when there was a far more tangible source of danger living in Plato's cave: the puppeteers. It was their job to fool the prisoners into thinking that shadows were real objects. What saved Plato's imaginary prisoner 2,500 years ago was not the sun. It was getting away from the puppeteers. Nevertheless, my college-aged self, my students, and Western history have mistakenly gleaned from Plato's story a fear of, and concomitant hatred for, darkness.

The problem is not the cave. The solution is not the light. Shadows exist in broad daylight too, and anyone who offers you the light of truth without the truth of darkness is selling you noontime pride and midnight shame.

Night Vision is not a bright-sided philosophy* about our dark moods. It won't ask you to be grateful for your grief or to love your anxiety. It's a social critique launched by six philosophers in de-fense of those moods. In the light, our dark moods make us look broken. In the dark, though, we look fully human. Each mood is a new set of eyes through which we can see a world that others

---

* Barbara Ehrenreich called out America's tendency to bully us into staying on the sunny side of life in *Bright-Sided: How the Relentless Promotion of Positive Thinking Has Undermined America* (2009). Her book was shortly followed by Oliver Burkeman's *The Antidote: Happiness for People Who Can't Stand Positive Thinking* (2013).

can't—or won't. Each philosopher in this book offers new words for our dark moods. And while you won't find any of them calling your depression a superpower, they do better than "You're lovable *despite* your disease." They understand that each of us is a unique ratio of dark to light, and that each combination is respectable, dignified, fully human. They can show us how to see in the dark.

Plato's successors taught us to evaluate dark moods by the light of science, psychology, and religion. I invite you to doubt your intellectual inheritance and consider the possibility that to find dignity in darker moods, you'll need to step *out* of the light and back into the cave. I take my cue from the novelist, environmentalist, and poet Wendell Berry, who wrote:

To go in the dark with a light is to know the light.
To know the dark, go dark. Go without sight,
and find that the dark, too, blooms and sings,
and is traveled by dark feet and dark wings.[4]

If Berry is right that dark moods are best known in the dark, let's stop shedding light on them.

We have all experienced dark moods. Some of us are living through one at this moment, and some are on the edge of one. Resisting the throng of best-selling puppeteers peddling their gratitude journals, let us head into the cave for the length of this book to learn what we can know in the dark. *Night Vision* is a way of seeing in the sense that it's a way of knowing. It includes feeling, imagining, judging, embodying, and thinking of all kinds. From now on, we will turn down the lights and stop smiling. We will suspend the idea that darkness is to be feared, minimized, or escaped. We will ignore the voices that say learning happens only in the light of day. There are no puppeteers here—only philosophers who have known anger, sadness, grief, depression, and anxiety.

chapter 1

getting honest about anger

If I had known that only one-third of US philosophy majors in college were women, I might not have majored in philosophy. If I had calculated that in ten years' time I would become one of only about twenty Latina professional philosophers in the United States, I might have bailed.[1] At the very least, I would have gotten angry at the fact that my academic discipline has the poorest diversity statistics among all the humanities. But I was still white back then.

Had I been Brown, I might not have gone to a mostly white college, or since I did, I probably would have been pointed to ethnic studies. Had I been Black, I might have been told that "philosophy is not for Black women," as happened to the sister of the professional philosopher Kristie Dotson not in 1969 but in 2009. The combined effect of my light skin color, middle-class background, Anglicized name (Mary), citizenship status, and heteronormative upbringing gave me access to the world of professional philosophy. Passing for white (and believing my Chilean grandmother that I was) helped me get the PhD. The first-generation US citizen Mary earned the right to shine in front of (mostly white male) philosophers at professional conferences.

It's only in the last ten years that I have questioned society's wholesale rejection of darkness and also begun taking seriously the suggestion made by various colleagues that I am a Woman of Color. My reluctance to embrace this category has come from not wanting to insult "real" Women of Color, whose darker skin or ethnic markers like language or accent block them from exclusive academic, economic, and social circles. (According to one compelling logic, "if you get to wonder whether you are a Woman of Color or not, then you're not!") But upon moving to South Texas on the US-Mexico border, I found myself growing darker in a variety of senses. I now use my family name, Mariana, because I finally live in a place where my name doesn't belly-flop off of nervous tongues. Since almost 90 percent of the population in the Rio Grande Valley is Hispanic or Latinx, my skin tone and Spanish fit right in. But I'll not forget that I got through the doors of philosophy as Mary, who still lives inside of Mariana. Together we got the PhD to make room for the next generation of Academics of Color. This book, which rejects the basic assumption that light—emotional and otherwise—is holier than dark, is a product of my experience of being both.

Philosophers of Color who faced philosophy's biases and still managed to earn a PhD—or their "philosophical passport," as one Mexican American scholar calls it—still encounter racism and discrimination.[2] Many of them, especially women, are run out of the academy despite having earned their place. Angela Davis, for example, was fired from the University of California at Los Angeles for being "too political." Joyce Mitchell Cook, the first Black woman to earn a PhD in the United States, was denied tenure by Howard, as was LaVerne Shelton by Rutgers and Adrian Piper by the University of Michigan. These Women of Color crossed the border of professional philosophy legally but were deported anyway. Others got so fed up that they left willingly. Some were granted asylum in other disciplines, like María Lugones, who we'll hear from shortly. Until she died in 2020, her home departments at Binghamton University were comparative literature and women, gender, and sexuality studies. In one way or another, academic philosophy bleeds its Women of Color.

When this happens, when Women of Color are dismissed from academic philosophy, their ideas—on anger and everything else—are not taken seriously. Kristie Dotson (whose sister the academic adviser tried to dissuade from studying philosophy) published an essay titled "How Is This Paper Philosophy?" in which she argues that Philosophers of Color—the ones who make it through the gauntlet described here—are still routinely forced to justify why their ideas should count as "real" philosophy.[3] It's infuriating. More to the point, it's indicative of a larger problem: a society that strains to associate dark skin with wisdom also has a hard time pairing a dark mood like "anger" with "healthy" or "justified."

For centuries, philosophers were the explicit storytellers of our souls. Even though now—let's be honest—philosophy is more like a trickle of ideas seeping out of the broken tiles that line windowless classrooms, what college students learn in their philosophy classes still reaches the public. And when it's mostly white, mostly cisgender, mostly heterosexual male professors teaching classrooms full of mostly white, mostly cisgender, mostly heterosexual male philosophers, what they teach about moods like anger is likely to reflect that reality. It's neither a surprise nor a coincidence that almost none of the ideas about anger circulating in philosophy classrooms—and by extension our society—have been provided by Women of Color.

In a hundred years, maybe our commonsense beliefs about anger will come from a distinguished line of Women of Color like Audre Lorde, bell hooks, and María Lugones, who make a case for listening to our anger. But today our views still come from the first major proponents of the Light Metaphor: ancient Greek and Roman philosophers. Their stories about how anger works and why it's bad have been dominant throughout history, and they're not very kind to angry women in the twenty-first century. In the light of their ancient philosophies, anger looks irrational, crazy, and ugly. Broken.

———

Plato compared passions like anger to a hard-to-control, hot-blooded, black-skinned horse that must be reined in by the "charioteer" of reason.[4] He thought we should use self-control to contain our anger, and he was not alone. The Roman Stoic Seneca, who described anger similarly, once told a story about Plato getting livid.[5] Instead of beating one of his slaves, as others would have done reflexively, Plato froze, his hand drawn back in striking position. A friend of his walked onto this scene and asked Plato what was going on. "I am making an angry man expiate his crime," Plato replied.[6] For Plato, rage is a sign that you are out of control. Although many people successfully use rage as an excuse to hurt others (those who commit "crimes of passion" often get shorter sentences than those who calmly and rationally carry out the same act), Plato's freezing was his way of acknowledging that rage is weakness. Seneca formulated Plato's example into a principle: the only appropriate time to express anger is when you are not angry. Otherwise, you're a slave to your emotion.

Many of us know people who get angry too often. Some of us are those people. The pandemic hit shortly after I had been granted a year of glorious leave from teaching and administrative responsibilities to write this book. I was supposed to have eight-hour days, five days a week, to write. But then schools closed, and suddenly I found myself admitting to my children's teachers that I didn't think "remote learning" was a good idea, especially for a first-grader. So I chose the lesser of two evils: ditching the iPads, I homeschooled my kids using books and pencils.

"I'm not your slave!" I yelled after I was interrupted for the fifth time in an hour. I was playing the piano, which is my thirty-minute version of alone time, but someone's Kindle needed charging. Before that, there were no good books on the Kindle. Before that, the Kindle was lost. I must have screamed, "I am a person!" seventy times since the Covid-19 quarantine had begun the previous year. More than once I fantasized about overturning my dining room table like I was a Real New Jersey Housewife. I imagined the satisfaction that would come from pushing my six-year-old into the wall, and then I immediately reprimanded myself. I knew I was not supposed to harm my children, but in those moments of fury I could not remember why. I longed to be freed from feeding my kids three times a day and educating them in the hopes that one day they would stop knocking at my bathroom door and go to college.

Later that night, I brusquely accused my husband of working in the garage so he would not have to put the kids to bed or hear them sneak out of their bedrooms and start jumping on my nerves. "Jesus Christ" escaped my mouth more times that month than in twelve pre-Covid months combined, and in every invective I uttered against the children, I heard my father's

voice shouting, "*Como se te occure?*" (What were you thinking?)
I closed my eyes and saw my mother slink down before him as
my children did before me now.

Growing up, I saw the anger of a father who predictably
pounded dinner tables. We knew it would happen, but not on
which nights, or why. The warning signs of his volcanic temper included three repeated moves: First he would grab at his
colossal nose with his right hand a few times in rapid succes-
sion. Then he would run that same hand through his full head
of white hair, all while sucking in air through his teeth: *click.*
At dinner, in the car, or in the grocery store, at the first sign
of nose-hair-click, you got ready. You'd look at the floor, keep
quiet, say "Yes, Papa" if, in his thick accent, he asked any rhetorical questions like "Do you know that I am your father?"
You would pray for the verbal eruption to be quick and not
to be too badly burned by it. I would shake but not cry.
I figured crying would make things worse, plus I did not want
him to win.

Like Plato and Seneca, I was frightened by anger, but because
I was a child when I first saw my father erupt, I also began to
smolder. Some children of angry parents go the other way, but
many of us become angry adults. All of us are, in some way,
dealing with the anger that we saw or did not see in our
childhood.

My first explanation for my Covid-anger was that I was a
monster. I was suspicious of that story, though. It smelled like
ancient philosophy. Even though Plato was not talking about
me (or any woman), all I had to do was look in a mirror to see
what he described: hair in tangles, wild, sunken eyes, clothes
askew. Lockdown had turned me into a dark horse running
amok. I did not want to become a permanently embittered
woman, lashing out at my children and husband over minor

infractions. But neither could I seem to stop the hot surge of fury from rising into my head and shooting off my tongue.

Like all mothers, I had absorbed messages from our society about how parents should and should not behave. Good moms do not frighten their children or ask them what's wrong with them. Good moms do not call kids selfish or brats or make them feel small. And it doesn't take sitting in a philosophy class to have inherited the ancient message: anger is shameful. In truth, shame only approximates what the angriest of us feel after a blowup. Angry women tend to lack compassion for themselves. Some of us go to self-help books. Being a professional philosopher, I sadomasochistically went back to my sources. I took a deeper look at my anger through all the lenses I'd loved; though they were the oldest and most outdated of sources, I was not alone in the surprising hold they still had over me.

To temper my Covid-anger, I turned to one of my favorite philosophers of light, the man who coined the idea that we could be happy if we worked hard enough. Epictetus was the Stoic philosopher whose short *Handbook* I used to read every year. For the fifteenth time, he told me that "an uneducated man blames others; a partially educated man blames himself. A fully educated man blames no one."[7] While I could not control my circumstances—Epictetus granted that I did not have the power to end a pandemic or reopen schools—I could control my bursts of anger. Instead of blaming my husband and kids for my troubles, I should blame myself for expecting life to be easier. Better yet, I should blame no one and accept the new normal gracefully. This sounded bootstrappy, American style. I liked it. After all, I'd grown up in New York City ("if you can make it here, you can make it anywhere") as a first-generation US citizen. I was taught to love hard work. So I kept at it.

I reread the *Meditations* of Marcus Aurelius, the second-century Roman emperor and Stoic who believed that yielding to anger is a sign of weakness.[8] Marcus reformulated one of the central tenets of Stoicism: "Disturbance comes only from within—from our own perceptions."[9] His advice? Lower your expectations. Remember that the only person you can change is yourself. To that end, expect people to irritate you daily and you will be ready for it.[10] For me that meant remembering that having kids meant having messes. I needed to stop being surprised or annoyed by it. But expecting a mess did not clean the table every night, load or unload the dishwasher, or vacuum the crumb-riddled floor. Marcus did not send his servants to clean my house. Cleaning lockdown messes reminded me of why I had abandoned Stoicism the first time I practiced it, nearly seven years earlier.

When my first son was born, I tried walking in the light of Stoicism. For the first year of my son's life, I told myself that humans control their feelings. Following Marcus's counsel, I trained myself to expect daily irritations. I imagined the causes of misery that I was likely to encounter so that, when I did encounter them, I would not be surprised. Sometimes it was helpful: picturing my six-month-old blowing out of his diaper made it easier for me to get on a plane with him than if, optimistically, I had been expecting tamer bowels.

Back then, I asked the Stoics to help me find a way to avoid getting mad at my sweet newborn when he cried for twenty-five hours a day instead of sleeping like the baby I had imagined. I tried the Stoic practice of *memento mori*: contemplating my own death in the hopes of being able to say, "The time goes so fast!" I tried journaling like Marcus, detailing my upsets and calming them with the pen. I tried "the view from above," in which you picture how small and insignificant this moment in your life is compared to your whole life and even the universe.[11] I walked, I read, I meditated. But even after expecting disappointment and envisioning myself as an insignificant bug in an oversized universe, I felt little relief. I still wanted to throw the crying bundle out the window. I never did it, but my inability to stop feeling angry was enough to keep me also feeling like a failure. I was too weak ("uneducated," whispered Epictetus) to live up to the standard set by the Stoics. So I left them for Aristotle.

Aristotle's philosophy worked better for me during the baby years. I appreciated his advice to not waste too much time trying to control my feelings, both because feelings come and go and also because they aren't nearly as important as actions. Instead of drawing our soul as a charioteer riding horses, as Plato did, Aristotle's picture reminded me of a popcorn tin divided into three flavors: *feelings, predispositions,* and *active conditions.* We have the most experience with feelings: happy, sad, mad, nervous, and so on. Feelings just happen, and while some are appropriate, like anger at injustice, some aren't as nice, like envy. Still, Aristotle said, feelings are hard to change, so let's not waste too much energy trying. Predispositions name the likelihood that we will feel those feelings. Some people lose their keys and burst into tears; others rage. People have different emotional predispositions.

If I had been predisposed to sadness, I might have cried during quarantine when my younger son refused to do his writing lesson. But since I am predisposed to anger, I told him to go to his room because I didn't want to look at him. But then I didn't want to look at me. How often I wished, in vain, that I could just cry when things fell apart, like "normal" people, sweet people, feminine people. Every night during lockdown,

Aristotle would put his arm around me and gently remind me that my predispositions did not determine my behavior.

Feelings and predispositions matter, Aristotle said, but only because it's a philosophical virtue to know yourself. It's helpful to know that I get mad easily and often, like every time a drawer is stuck or a box of Entenmann's doughnuts refuses to yield at the tabs. Some of us pride ourselves on being in touch with our feelings—and Aristotle would applaud us—but then he'd quickly usher us onto the main stage: behavior.

Aristotle believed that it's most important to cultivate the right "active conditions," to control how we "bear" ourselves in the face of feelings and predispositions. Forever a fan of right action, he suggested that we train our souls to react beautifully even to an ugly mess. There have been times when, instead of threatening my younger son with a punishment for not getting dressed, I have helped his weary body walk over to the dresser to pick out clothes. This is beautiful action. Why shame myself for feeling angry when I had Aristotle letting me be angry so long as I acted beautifully? Angry feelings are useful, he believed, because they give us a chance to practice behaving well despite feeling the urge to throw it all away. Many of us are Aristotelian without knowing it, and it can make us feel like a hero to almost do something ugly but choose to act beautifully instead.

Unlike the Stoics, Aristotle mercifully rejected "shoulds" when it comes to feelings, since feelings are natural and harmless if we do not act on them. Feeling angry enough to want to defenestrate a baby is natural enough, but what was important to Aristotle was my refusing to follow through on that impulse. Feeling angry and resentful when you are burdened with homeschooling on top of working and chores is acceptable, but venting that anger is not. As Mister Rogers so charmingly put

Aristotle's point, "Everyone has lots of ways of feeling. And all of those feelings are fine. It is what we do with our feelings that matters in this life."[12]

Sadly, though, during lockdown even Aristotle's less judgmental mountain looked too high for me to climb. Even though he gave me permission to feel angry so long as I didn't act angrily, I got tired of behaving beautifully. His philosophy had gotten me through the baby years, but it was not helpful anymore. His views on anger made me sweat when I failed to stop myself from throwing a handful of roasted almonds at each kid once when they were bickering over who got more. I started to see Aristotle not as my sweetheart but as a father figure telling me: *It's okay to flirt with darkness, just don't marry it.* I was determined to rebel.

My experience with lockdown anger left me caught between two bright lights: the Stoics, who told me I should not let myself get angry, and Aristotle, who said I could get angry so long as I didn't act on it. I even tried Pythagoras's advice to "counter rage with melody" by listening to Debussy and Alice in Chains.[13] But every time I had what the Greeks called a "temper tantrum" I felt like something was deeply wrong with me.[14] The haggard-looking woman stuck in the house looking at me in the mirror *was* ugly, irrational, and crazy. So said the ancients, and with their words echoing in my head, so said I. I was hearing the Brokenness Story.

Every time we call anger "irrational," "ugly," or "crazy," we are invoking ancient philosophers just as surely as if we went around saying that anger means we are possessed by demons or that we suffer from an excess of yellow bile.[15] The ancients' Light Metaphor dominates bookshelves to this day. In *The Subtle Art of Not Giving a F*ck: A Counterintuitive Approach to Living a Good Life*, Mark Manson says that we can decide what to give a f*ck about, just as the Stoics believed. Like the Stoics, he leans hard on choice: we get to decide what we value, how we handle adversity, and what it all means. If life leaves a steaming bag of sh*t on our doorstep, Manson says, it may not be our fault, but it is our responsibility.[16] On his reading, I could have decided *not* to take my kids' disrespect personally. I didn't *have* to let other people rile me up. Manson denies that he is participating in the historical revival of Stoic philosophy (since 2012)—which includes the blog Stoicism Today, Ryan Holiday and Stephen Hanselman's *The Daily Stoic*, and the public events Stoic Week and Stoicon— but his books suggest otherwise.[17] The demographic most attracted to Stoicism today—the one that has earned it the cheeky moniker "Broicism"—is the same one Manson seems to be targeting with his expletive-filled "straight talk."

In Aristotle's corner, Gary Bishop's *Stop Doing That Sh*t* talks about how we can feel bad but do it anyway.[18] ("It" being the duty required. For example, I've told a cranky kid: "It's okay to be mad/sad about having to ride your bike home. Cry if you want to—while peddling.") According to this philosophy, it doesn't matter how much you are up against—you still have the power to control your behavior. Gary Bishop still expects you to get a hold of yourself, *goddammit*.

Whether you believe you can stop yourself from getting angry (like the Stoics) or you believe you can get angry as long as you don't act on it (like Aristotle), chances are good that you inherited from the ancient Greeks and Romans a bias against anger. But turning away from it is not going to help you see it more clearly.

Aristotle and the Stoics may have shed different lights on my almond-throwing at the dinner table, but they agreed that I needed to calm down. I agreed in theory, but some part of me was infuriated by the suggestion. I recalled the story of

Alexander the Great taming his wild horse Bucephalus by forcing him to stare at the sun. The horse was afraid of his own shadow, and staring at the light stopped him from spooking. But it also blinded him and made him obedient. Like many women, when I calm down, I end up concluding that whatever I was in a huff about was not a big deal, that I must have overreacted. Like Bucephalus, I do not fight back. I obey.

The ancient Greek and Roman philosophers did not tell us to listen to our anger. They did not leave us a helpful lens through which to see or challenge structural injustices that are making us so angry. Neither does today's self-help industry. Self-help was not designed to widen the too-narrow hallways of our existence. It promises only to help us live our best life once we accept that the studs won't budge. But what if we believed they could?

During the pandemic, women lost a million more jobs than men. Black, Latina, and Asian women lost the most out of everybody. We can fight to change this world—to widen the hallways of existence for Women of Color—but we never will if we are convinced in advance that our anger is irrational, ugly, or crazy. Feeling guilty about feeling angry has kept too many of us distracted and obedient.

It is time for a demolition and rebuild, a renovation in our thinking about anger and a widening of the emotional walls that surround us. We can start by giving ourselves more room to be angry. What would change if we derived our ideas about anger, not from ancient Greek and Roman men, but from twentieth-century Women of Color? What if we made Women of Color our guides in the cave of anger? What could they help us see?

Audre Lorde might be the first woman in modern history to explicitly stand behind her anger and to insist that, without anger, we will not get anywhere. Before Lorde, early anger pioneers included the former slave Sojourner Truth, whose angry "Ain't I a Woman?" speech at the National Women's Rights Convention in Ohio in 1851 made plain the difference between how white and Black women were treated; Ida B. Wells Barnett, who in 1892 publicly and angrily exposed the lynching of Blacks in Memphis; and Rosa Parks, who in 1955 called her anger a case of being "tired." In 1981, when Lorde was already a well-respected literary figure in the Black community, she gave a legendary speech in which she complained about being asked to modify her tone to make listeners feel more comfortable. Lorde was indignant that the wrong people are constantly asked to speak more softly when they really need to get louder. She birthed a philosophical alternative to the ancient scripts by refusing to call anger irrational.

Audre Lorde was born in Harlem in 1934, the third daughter of West Indian immigrants. She excelled in writing and rebellion, to the dismay of her strict mother, who was embarrassed by her "wild child" daughter. Lorde's mother was light-skinned and could pass for non-Black. Perhaps that was why she looked down on darker-skinned Blacks, the "others," who ate black-eyed peas and watermelon. At the same time, although the Lorde family did not talk about racial injustice, Audre got the message that neither were whites their allies.

Mr. and Mrs. Lorde tried to shield their children from the ugliness of racism, perhaps in an effort to rise above it, but on a trip to Washington, DC, they could hide from it no longer. After a visit to a historical museum, the Lordes were refused service at an ice-cream parlor. No one explained to Audre why she couldn't have ice cream. Nor did her family help her make sense of what was going on in the United States. Between their opacity about racism and her strict upbringing, Audre only became wilder.

Mrs. Lorde might have thought that raising her children to feel suspicious of whites and superior to Blacks would give them an advantage in life, but Audre would not copy her mother's prejudices. Instead of inheriting her mother's bias against both dark and light skin, Audre surrounded herself with men and women of all shades. And she stood up for herself, first in the poetry she wrote at Hunter High School, and later in the poetry she published while she was a philosophy minor at Hunter College.[19]

At age forty-seven, Lorde gave "The Uses of Anger" as a keynote speech at the National Women's Studies Association conference in Connecticut. The first step to understanding anger, according to Lorde, was to stop fearing it. "My fear of anger taught me nothing," said Lorde. "Your fear of that anger will teach you nothing, also."[20]

It seems only natural to fear anger, since it can be so destructive. Seneca had come by his fear of anger honestly: as adviser to Nero, the very angry and crazy child emperor, he had witnessed a man burning a city down for fun. I have feared anger since I realized I lived under the roof of an angry father. You might fear anger too, if you have seen too much or too little of it. Not fearing anger takes some doing, but if Lorde is right, it is necessary for progress.

"Focused with precision," Lorde told her audience, anger "can become a powerful source of energy serving progress and change."[21] Before 1981, fewer voices paired anger with progress and change, and the ones who did, like Malcolm X, were portrayed in the press as dark and dangerous. For those of us who are used to associating anger with danger, pairing it with progress and change takes extra work.

Lest we worry that anger will make us haters, Lorde insisted on the difference between anger and hatred. Her speech about anger was directed against racism, she said, not against people. "Hatred is the fury of those who do not share our goals. Its object is death and destruction."[22] Lorde would say that the bombing of abortion clinics is not anger in action, it's hatred. Getting angry about a policy that removes immigrant children from the arms of their parents, however, is not hatred. "Its object is change."[23] Lorde insisted that we learn to differentiate between anger and hatred, so that we can be on guard against people who mix them up.

The contemporary philosopher Myisha Cherry coined the term "Lordean rage" to describe anger targeted at racism.[24] But we can extend Lorde's defense of anger to other cases, like demanding equal pay for female athletes, closing the gender-empathy gap (people perceiving men to be in more pain than women), respecting and supporting neurodiversity, or demanding rights for incarcerated individuals. Anything that has justice at its core is Lorde's kind of anger.

Getting mad does not always make us right, but neither does it make us irrational. Whatever else anger is, it is also, as Lorde said, "loaded with information and energy."[25] If we dismiss our anger because we think it must be irrational, we will never listen to it. If we turn against ourselves, we will not find out what our anger is trying to tell us.

Many of us, in the heat of an angry outburst, get told to calm down. In her speech, Lorde recounted an experience of being at an academic conference and speaking "out of direct and particular anger." An unnamed white woman responded to Lorde's anger by saying, "Tell me how you feel but don't say it too harshly or I cannot hear you."[26] I have been tone-policed too, and it is insidiously distracting. The person you are talking to shifts attention from what you are saying to how you are saying it. When an angry woman gets tone-policed, she is being reminded to be ashamed of her anger, to know her place. In a world flooded with light, there is no room for darkness. Those invested in the status quo, the puppeteers, will call her irrational, and they will even shut her up by force, if necessary. Plato thought acting in anger was irrational. The Stoics thought it was crazy. Aristotle thought it was ugly. Caught in these ancient lights, you are not very likely to be able to stand up to the tone-police if they come for you. You will probably back down, rephrase, or let it go. As a bonus, you might also feel ashamed of having "let yourself" get angry (thanks, Stoics). My anger has often left me feeling broken and weak, wishing I were tamer. For many of us in the United States, the feeling of anger provokes shame, which only deepens if we express it.

Lorde did not surrender to the tone-police. Instead, she wondered if the white woman who called out her anger did so because she could not bear to hear the words Lorde was saying. Listening would have required changing.[27] To the tone-police worldwide, Lorde announced: "I cannot hide my anger to spare you guilt, nor hurt feelings, nor answering anger, for to do so insults and trivializes all our efforts."[28] If Lorde had believed that her anger was irrational, she would never have dared to take up space in the conference room that day. Lorde's belief in her anger's rationality empowered her to seek justice.

A society that equates a woman's strength with her capacity to bottle up her grievances, a society that admonishes us with the perennial reminder that someone else has it worse, a society that hands her a self-help book instead of admitting that she has a raw deal, is a society full of sick women. In *Rage Becomes Her*, the anger expert Soraya Chemaly discusses a study that found that "anger is the single, most salient emotional contributor to pain."[29] And because women suffer more silently than men, Chemaly concludes, anger affects women's bodies in ways we have not even realized yet.[30] What my sweet Minnesotan cousin has been calling "chronic pelvic pain" might also very well be repressed anger. After all, we've learned that when we swallow anger it does not disappear. We have also heard that when we express it (as boys are more often encouraged to), we survive. In one study cited by Chemaly, breast cancer patients who expressed their anger survived at twice the rate of those who kept it in.[31]

The anger Lorde described in her speech was intensely dark. It was also methodical, clearheaded, and calculative—just as we become when we have to move about in the dark. Lorde was asking us to trust ourselves and to use our anger as a tool with which to "excavate honesty" from ourselves and our world.[32] We can't dig for truth with our bare hands. We need anger to be the spade that breaks ground and scoops dirt to this and that side of an issue. We can get to the truth only if we learn to use our tool instead of assuming it is something to hide.

Even those of us who, agreeing with Lorde, have begun to make small efforts to link "anger" with "tool" and "honesty" are still likely to get weighed down by the two other millstones bequeathed to us by the ancient philosophy of light: "crazy" and "ugly."

———

On January 6, 2021, hundreds of people, mostly white men, broke into the US Capitol Building to "stop the steal," that is, to prevent Joe Biden from being officially declared the winner of the 2020 presidential election. The world watched as protesters gained ground, first breaking through police barricades to over-run the steps of the Capitol, then gaining access to the building by breaking windows and bodies. I was not the only viewer expecting the mob's violence to be met in kind by the police. We held our collective breath as we waited for the clubs and guns to come out, but we saw no rioters get beaten by the police that day. Instead of seeing injured criminals getting carried out on stretchers, we saw hundreds of smiling folks being escorted out of the building like audience members being funneled through double doors after attending a Broadway show. No angry rioter was arrested inside the building, and by the end of the day only fifty-two people had been arrested, mostly for violating the 5:00 PM curfew.[33] A day later, the FBI put out cash-incentivized calls seeking help in locating the individuals allowed by police to "do their thing" the day before.[34] This made many of us ask why the police had not arrested them while they were in the building. Why did they let the protesters go?

The confused among us were used to seeing video footage of police beating up Black people. We had seen four thousand armed members of the National Guard in army fatigues "protect" the steps of the Lincoln Memorial during a Black Lives Matter protest six months earlier.[35] We had read about stun grenades, rubber bullets, sting guns, tear gas, pepper spray, and batons being used against protesters after the murder of George Floyd.[36] We had heard about the thousands of arrests made that night and in the decades since the civil rights movement, not for crushing police officers' windpipes but for sitting down.[37]

The Light Metaphor—which on a billboard looks like a white woman with a glowing smile and on the TV show *Cops* looks like a Black man getting restrained—has made it harder to see white anger as dangerous. "Capitol Assault a More Sinister Attack than First Appeared," an Associated Press headline read.[38] What was it about an angry mob breaking the windows of the Capitol Building that did not look sinister at first glance? To whom? One man at the protest carried a pitchfork—a symbol of violence committed against Black bodies following the Emancipation; another took a Confederate flag inside, and a good number of the rioters were shattering glass. They had weapons on them: guns, knives, pipes, and restraints. They set up a gallows inside the building and shouted, "Hang Mike Pence!"[39] They stashed bombs around the building. What part of a sweatshirt that says MAGA CIVIL WAR JANUARY 6, 2021 gave the impression that these folks came in peace?

Since the attack, people have speculated that if the rioters had been Black, they would have been shot.[40] To be clear, there was no red carpet laid out for the white Capitol rioters to enter, but neither was their anger immediately (or ever, in some cases) interpreted as crazy or dangerous.

The Stoics would deny that anger is reasonable, including the anger of the Capitol rioters. Aristotle would have scolded the behavior, not the feelings. Who wins in this debate? It might depend on which media you follow. For many viewers and participants, Aristotle won. It wasn't the anger that was wrong, commentators said, it was the behavior that the anger motivated. Even one of the rioters, who was later tracked down by a reporter, admitted that "things got out of hand."[41] He did not concede that his anger was crazy, just his behavior. If the rioters had been Black, maybe the Stoics would have won. Maybe viewers would have believed that the anger itself was crazy, not just the actions taken in the name of anger.

In *Killing Rage* (1995), the American author and philosopher bell hooks criticizes the 1968 book *Black Rage*, which is a psychological portrait of the Black male temperament. Hooks complains that although the authors are Black, they

still try to "convince readers that rage was merely a sign of pow-
erlessness."[42] She argues that Black male anger is routinely
pathologized or called sick, whereas white male anger is often
considered to be justified by circumstances (like the Capitol
riots, I would add).[43] We should consider the idea, hooks suggests, that Black anger has never been given a fair shake. As long
as we associate pathology with darkness, we won't be able to see
Black anger as hooks sees it—as a "potentially healthy, potentially healing response to oppression and exploitation."[44]

Lorde believed that anger is informative and rational, to
which hooks would add that it is potentially healthy. They both
helped me see that when I got Covid-angry from being interrupted by my kids, I was mistaken to get angry at them for need-
ing help, and I was wrong to make them feel like a burden. But
by treating Lorde and hooks as my philosophers of anger instead of Aristotle and the Stoics, I learned that I should not have
judged my anger before hearing it out.

If I had listened to my anger, I would have been able to use it
to "excavate honesty," to ask what was really going on in my
house. From now on, I told myself, I will listen to my anger. I
will see my dark mood as an ally trying to give me information.
I will no longer assume my own irrationality or madness, and
I will hold my angry head up a little higher.

There was still one problem left: I felt ugly angry. The Light
Metaphor says that angry women are ugly compared to women
who say, "Can't complain!" about their unbearable circumstances and who get called beautiful, sunny, bright.

In the 1970s, calling a feminist ugly was a great way to avoid
taking her ideas seriously. It's a cheap but effective tactic: focus-
ing on a woman's physical appearance instead of listening to her
words is a way of dissolving her message. The Argentinean

philosopher María Lugones did not seem to care if she was perceived as ugly or not. I once saw her eat a pear whole: skin, seeds, core. Compared to my Chilean mother, who eats a pear delicately, skinning it with a knife and then cutting it into little pieces to be eaten with a dessert fork, Lugones looked like an animal. Maybe it was her way of bucking convention—thumbing her nose at civilization—or maybe she did not want to waste food. Either way, she took the risk of looking barbaric as she trusted her body to absorb the fruit's nutrients and flush out its waste. By then she had learned to trust her mind to sort the good from the bad of what she called her "hard to handle anger."[45]

Unlike Audre Lorde and bell hooks, Lugones was not always a defender of anger. More like Seneca watching Rome burn, Lugones had reason to be skeptical about anger. In her youth she saw the kind of anger that manifests as violence: "I relocated to the United States from violence. My location is that of someone who relocated away from battering, systematic rape, extreme psychological and physical torture, by those closest to me. I relocated in the sense of going for a new geographical place, a new identity, a new set of relations."[46] In the 1960s, Lugones fled from Argentina to the United States, where she earned her bachelor's degree and then her PhD in philosophy. She taught at Carleton College from 1972 to 1994 before moving to Binghamton University, where she was teaching until her death in 2020.[47]

Lugones worried about what anger said about her, who it made her: "On the one hand, I find myself angrier and angrier; on the other, I have always disliked being overwhelmed by emotion."[48] Lugones's inner conflict is familiar to many of us. During a hot angry spell, we might feel like Wile E. Coyote, who has already run past the cliff's edge but whose feet keep on cycling. When we realize we have gone too far, we regret having left solid ground. We wish to rejoin the land of nice people.

"Most of all," Lugones wrote, "I have disliked myself in deep overwhelming anger."[49] Few angry women can look in the mirror while they are enraged and like what they see. More than sadness or anxiety, anger tends to make us feel ugly. Maybe it's because anger is a stereotypically masculine emotion that we are not supposed to feel, let alone express. Maybe Lugones did feel ugly. Maybe she had been raised to keep her anger in check and to eat a pear "like a lady": skinning it, cutting it up, and discarding its coarse parts.

And yet, as women get increasingly angry, we are starting to resent the knee-jerk assumption that it's ugly. We are starting to realize that even though a woman's angry demand to be heard at a business meeting may look ugly, it isn't necessarily so. By retraining our eyes to see in the dark, we might one day conclude that our anger is beautiful. In time, though, when we have really progressed, we will step beyond the merely aesthetic realm, as we already do for some groups. We don't typically call a white man's anger ugly or beautiful; we only ask if it's justified.

Lugones offers three pieces of wisdom about anger in the dark:

First, stop talking about anger in the singular. Lugones was not the first philosopher to suggest that anger has many names. The Greeks distinguished between angers and gave each its own term. *Nemesis* is the daughter of Justice. She flies around, dagger in hand, making things right. She rights wrongs. She demands restitution and gives the hurt party what they are due.[50] *Orgē* is intense anger that borders on madness, the one that Seneca and Cicero were so afraid of. There is also *mēnis* (wrath), *chalepaino* (annoyance), *kotos* (resentment), and *cholos* (bitterness, from "bile").[51] Not only are there different terms describing different angers, but in the Greek some of them are portrayed as spirited feelings instead of downers.[52] When Lugones reminds us that there are multiple angers, she is tapping into a long tradition that we have forgotten, one that at least respected anger's diversity.

The idea that there are various angers explains a lot. It explains why some people can still feel ugly even while agreeing with Lorde that anger is a healthy and rational political tool. The nagging voice in my head that reminds me of how nervous I used to get going to the dinner table as a child, the voice assuring me that I inherited my father's anger, is not always wrong. My anger sometimes does damage to my kids and sometimes to myself. Simply reversing positions on anger and concluding that dark is the new light will not help. Taking our cue from Lugones, we might start talking about *kotos* versus *nemesis* instead of just "their anger" versus "our anger." It's not true that rage is rage is rage: each anger needs to be studied for its history, source, effect, and productivity to determine whether it is ugly or not.

The idea that there are many angers also explains how a person could conclude that the anger of the Capitol rioters was ugly. Such a conclusion is not just a smoke-and-mirrors product of anti-anger propaganda. The trick is to acknowledge our angers as complex and not to disrespect their complexity by robotically stifling them or detonating them all over police officers and government buildings.

Second, Lugones agreed with Lorde that some angers are "full of information." Lugones had observed women in "hard to handle anger" who she said were also "outrageously clearheaded."[53] Their words rang "clean, true, undiluted by regard for others' feelings or possible reactions."[54] Have you ever been so angry that your mind clears? When you stop spending energy managing how you sound, you can use that energy to find the right words. I am often most articulate when my anger surpasses my concern for optics.

Finally, Lugones left us two philosophical categories to help us see anger more clearly. They are not types of anger like *nemesis* and *thumos*, but rather two ways to use anger. The first she calls *first-order* anger. It is "resistant, measured, communicative, and backward looking."[55] First-order anger is meant to be heard and understood.

You expressed first-order anger as a child when someone stole your toy and you screamed, "It's not fair!" You use it when you need to communicate something to someone who may not know what is going on but who would believe you if you could adequately articulate your complaint. First-order anger describes the anger of the Capitol rioters. But it also describes the anger of Black Lives Matter protesters. Both groups claim to seek justice, and both parties have a point to make. We cannot know ahead of time if first-order anger is virtuous—that will depend on reasoning, evidence, and precedents—but it is always communicative. First-order anger is always trying to tell us something. The trick is that it makes sense only to people who are willing to listen and/or who speak the same language. For people who don't get the argument of Black Lives Matter protesters, for example, the anger is nonsensical, literally. Critics cannot make sense of why Black people are so upset. Of course, some of them don't try, caught up as they are in the narrative that Black anger is crazy.

When a woman communicates first-order anger and her demand to be heard is rejected, *second-order anger* can flare up. If your anger has ever started off as measured but becomes increasingly desperate and loud as you realize that the person you are talking to is not listening or does not care, you may have strayed into second-order anger. When you feel you're not being understood, you try to make yourself clearer, to articulate your argument with more precision. Surely, you assume, the other person will hear you if you speak more clearly. But when even that does not work—when the effort exerted has left you sweating from mental strain, emotional energy, and wasted faith—you might find yourself "going off." With Lugones near, though, you need not be ashamed of this moment anymore. Your anger is simply adopting a different aim: self-protection.

Second-order anger is not about communicating anything. Lugones described it as "resistant, raging, uncommunicative, and forward looking."[56] You use it when first-order anger fails to be heard, understood, or paid attention to, when you are getting painted as ranting and raving. If the person you are talking to cannot see or understand the reason for your anger and instead calls you "crazy" or "emotional," then hope for communication is typically lost. You have been cast as an emotion rather than as a person with a coherent claim. Here's where second-order anger can help.

Lugones called second-order anger a "knowing experience" rather than a communicative one. She called it a form of self-care.[57] In second-order anger, you are no longer trying to convince anyone that your anger is justified. You stop declaring that you deserve better, that the world is sexist, that you need a break or are fed up. Second-order anger protects us from a world in which we do not make sense to the people we wish we made sense to. It is the anti-masker in the heat of Covid blowing up as she's escorted out of the grocery store. She is saying words but has lost hope of being understood, so instead she writhes, trying to insulate herself from a perceived injustice.

Second-order anger is intent on resisting a world where she shows up as crazy, the very world her friend, boss, or fellow shoppers are trying to convince her is the one she occupies. She is wrapping herself in the darkness of anger to get out of the blinding light of social convention. Just like first-order anger, second-order anger is not necessarily virtuous, but it can be.

We employ second-order anger when we are in danger of believing we are crazy.[58] Upon realizing that you literally do not make sense to a person or group, you stop communicating and start preserving your sanity. When a woman is gaslit—told there is no cause for her anger when there is—the last thing she needs is to believe that her anger is irrational, crazy, or ugly. Calling an angry woman any of these things is an attempt to shame her into conformity. Second-order anger rejects shame, thus allowing us to stay on our own side. Instead of allowing ourselves to be convinced that we are being nonsensical, second-order anger shuts out the nonbelieving world. In second-order anger, you might be screaming and wagging your finger, but your verbalizations and gestures are not intended as communication with others but as a means of driving naysayers away and protecting yourself from them.

The clearer we can get on what kind of anger we are feeling— first-order *nemesis*, or second-order *kotos*—the better we will be at knowing how to use it. "Know thyself" is an ancient philosophical commandment that still holds today. Recognizing and naming our angers can help us see which are good and which are bad, which are useful responses to injustice and which are fear in disguise. If I am employing first-order *nemesis* in my interaction with another person, it means that I think I can gain traction by talking to that person about the injustice. If I am employing second-order *kotos*, then it means I'm aware at some level of my resentment at not being taken seriously.

Having inherited a large sum of anger from my father, I once distrusted all my angers. But by listening to Lugones, I have come to see that not all of my angers are ugly. Some just need to be trained.

When Aristotle suggested that we train our anger, he meant for us to learn to control it. This is the kind of advice you will get when you shine a light on a dark emotion like anger. Anger management techniques, according to Soraya Chemaly, were devised to control "destructive, monstrous rage," or what we think of as "men's anger." The ancients were not studying women's anger, nor are many anger experts doing so today. Conceiving of anger in only the typically masculine way inevitably leads to the conclusion that anger needs to be controlled and managed.[59] "For women," Chemaly writes, "healthy anger management doesn't require us to exert more control but, rather, less. We are managing anger all the time without even realizing it."[60]

Since my Covid-anger coincided with my writing of this chapter, I challenged myself to sit in the dark with it until I could see something new. I began by calling my anger "poison," as per usual, and regurgitating the cliché that it was tearing my family apart. I had reached a familiar place. Angry people carry around a lot of shame. The difference was that this time I was not alone in the dark. I had Lorde, hooks, and Lugones sitting right next to me.

After hours of thinking and writing and dwelling in the darkness of my anger, I finally saw what I had been unable to see in the light. I said it out loud: "I'm burnt out."

Saying I was burnt out was entirely different from saying I was broken. Being broken means something on the *inside* is busted, like a water pipe bursting behind Sheetrock. Being burnt out means something on the *outside* is hurting us, like the exterior bricks of a house eroding from too much water exposure. The trouble is that many of us cannot make this distinction: when we sense rot, we have been conditioned to assume that it's coming from the inside—that it's us.

Philosophers have a specialized term for the discrediting of certain voices: *epistemic injustice.*[61] Epistemic *justice* takes place when someone who knows something is seen as a knower and treated like they know things. Epistemic injustice takes place when someone who knows something is not seen as a knower. In the United States, where Women of Color routinely face epistemic injustice, it has been nearly impossible to convince the community of professional philosophers who have always paired "knowledge" with "light" and "men" to start pairing it with "dark" and "women." Because I was raised in the United States, where ancient philosophies still dominate, I was taught to think that feeling anger meant I was broken, PMS-ing, sick. I was taught to distrust my anger. I believed the Brokenness Story.

At the beginning of the lockdown period of the pandemic, I had seen headlines about how women were not faring well—variations on "Women Are Breaking Down." Many of these commenters seemed to imply that women were too emotionally fragile for the pandemic. Maybe the "weaker sex" was too sensitive about rising death tolls. Maybe our pipes were bursting from too many tears.

As time went on, though, I started seeing articles detailing the poor working conditions of women in lockdown, who were expected to oversee the remote learning of their children while also working full-time from home. Studies of two-income households in the United States had shown that women already did more than their share of the domestic work and got paid less for outside work, but as the pandemic swelled, the domestic demands made on women only increased. To manage these demands women scaled back on or left the workforce at record rates. These articles helped me see that I was overburdened. My body was saying no—and in retrospect, loudly and clearly. Getting out from under the light of ancient philosophy also helped.

When I decided to trust in Lorde, hooks, and Lugones, they helped me stay on my own side. I identified my anger as the "knowing" kind of anger that Lugones talks about. It was recognizing and resisting the extra expectations being placed on me. My anger had been taking the form of second-order *kotos*—resentment at my unfair situation with no intention of trying to communicate. Listening to my anger helped. Instead of wasting another minute berating myself, I began requesting, demanding, and creating more time for myself. I began communicating my needs, transforming second-order anger into first-order anger. Fortunately, I was able to secure satisfaction. I stopped doing the dishes, cut the homeschooling demands in half, and got a three-day reprieve from childcare by asking my in-laws to watch our children.

Not everyone will get the relief their anger is demanding. But to turn against your anger simply because you cannot secure satisfaction would be a mistake. Anger functions to protect us, to keep us grounded in the reality of our unfair situation. To anyone who says that anger is useless if you cannot change your situation, Lorde, hooks, and Lugones would disagree. One of anger's functions is to preserve dignity. Women who are married to partners who tone-police or gaslight them might shift their anger from first-order, in which they hope to get results, to second-order, in which they give up on satisfaction but preserve their sanity. Knowing this difference could help them decide whether to stay or go.

If we keep listening to the merchants of light telling us that anger is, by default, ugly, crazy, and irrational, we will lose a means of fighting for justice. If we do not take shelter with Lorde, Lugones, and hooks, we are in danger of losing ourselves and our chance to see in the dark. We'll continue to turn on ourselves, wondering if the light promoters are right that we like to be negative. To stay on our own side we'll need to learn to replace "What's wrong with me?" with "What's wrong with my situation?" Those of us who are still tempted to look inward, to find the leak in ourselves, need only go outside and have a look around. Someone or something is holding a hose on us, and they're benefiting from our shame.

Since I had come to doubt my anger so fiercely and from such a young age, it has not been easy to learn to trust it. For those of you who do not get angry easily, it will probably feel wrong at first. But respecting our angers frees us to launch some critiques outward, critiques that would be available to us had we not been silenced by shame. The time I spent trying to quiet my anger and berating myself for not being able to was time spent not listening to a story of rotten gender dynamics in my home and society. To see some of our angers as dignified and even possibly justified, we will need to begin training them to work for us, as Lugones encouraged us to do, instead of taking Aristotle's advice to control them.[62]

At this point in history, it's undeniable that we are angry, even those of us who think otherwise. This realization leaves us with a choice—not whether to get angry or not, but whether to turn it inward or outward, to train it or to suffer the consequences of not training it. The next time we find ourselves in the dark of anger, let's try not calming down, counting to ten, or punching a pillow. Let's not breathe or do yoga in order to get into a better mood. Let's stay in the dark for an hour or two and listen to our anger.

We will not be alone. Black Lives Matter grew out of an appreciation for anger. Despite the fact that the work of Audre Lorde and bell hooks is not widely known yet, they have re-educated a handful of contemporary anger advocates. Soraya Chemaly, Brittney Cooper, Myisha Cherry, Rebecca Traistor, and Austin Channing Brown all reject the Brokenness Story, and they are helping us realize that the darkness of anger is an appropriate reaction to injustice. Even though the Buddha taught that anger causes suffering and needs to be abandoned, the dharma teacher and contemporary Buddhist Lama Rod Owens made space for anger in his 2020 book *Love and Rage: The Path of Liberation through Anger*.[63] This new generation of anger activists reminds us that seeking justice involves voicing our dissatisfaction, even when it displeases critics in and outside of our homes. And although anger is not a pleasant emotion, the least we can do is challenge the assumption that it's crazy, irrational, and ugly. If we can avoid feeling self-doubt on top of anger, we can use our anger more efficiently and stop it from "corroding our insides," in the words of Howard Thurman.[64]

Many years before these contemporary, angry activists published their first books, though, we had Audre Lorde, bell hooks, and María Lugones showing us what anger looks like in the dark. If you are convinced by this Trio of Color that anger is a personal and political tool—if you want to stay on your own side, that is—you can get busy excavating honesty in your heart, and, just as importantly, transforming society. Do not ignore or repress your anger. Because of the legacy of these women, those of us who have traditionally not been allowed to get angry, much less express it, have a chance to know anger in the dark. Once we agree to sit in anger instead of turning on a light, we will see that the ancient philosophies that have kept us under a heat lamp for almost 2,500 years did not know us or our anger when they said we were wrong to feel or express it.

In the dark, we can see that people who have the most legitimate anger are often the first to be called irrational, crazy, and ugly. In the dark, we can see that anger is to be trained, not suppressed or managed. Listen to your anger. Study it. Name it. Use it to "excavate honesty." And then pass on the wisdom of Lorde, hooks, and Lugones to anyone you meet who has been fed a diet of Color-less philosophy.

chapter 2

i suffer, therefore i am

A stranger at the park once told me, as I held my crying toddler, that children only cry harder if you acknowledge their pain, so it's best left ignored. As a child, I remember hearing talk of "wallowing" or having a "pity party." I'd overhear these same people telling their kids, "You get what you get, and you don't get upset." Children who heard these sorts of things were raised on the understanding that no one wants to hear where it hurt or to see them cry. Growing up in such a cold world could be one reason some of us are reluctant to broadcast our physical, emotional, or psychological pain.

In the United States, the rise of depression has been so disconcerting to the psychiatric community that other difficult moods, including "intense sadness," have been overlooked.[1] Sadness is real, they argue, and it's worth studying. But upon inspection, sadness starts to slip around theoretically and linguistically. Sadness has physical elements, but also psychological and emotional ones. Sadness and pain are often synonyms, but not always. In general, ambiguous moods cause people to crave simplicity. Early readers of this chapter on pain broadly conceived kept asking: But aren't you talking about worry here? Aren't you now talking about physical pain? Isn't this just sadness?

I mean to zoom out far enough to see where physical and emotional distress converge, where worry, sadness, and pain fuse. As a bilingual philosopher, I have chosen a Spanish word to mark this complicated gray area that resists a simplistic English translation. In Spanish, the word *dolor* refers to physical pain as well as to its emotional cousins grief, sadness, suffering, sorrow, distress, and depression. The lines between emotional and physical, or psychical and psychological, have never been as clear as we might like, but the word *dolor* crosses these borders easily. You can have a *dolor* in your ankle or your heart, your tooth or your soul. A recently divorced woman may describe herself as feeling *dolor* over her marriage ending. My three-year-old who cried when his father went to work was feeling *dolor*. When, at the age of eight, a toothpick impaled the bottom of my foot, I too felt *dolor*.

The woman who pulled out the toothpick—some friend's mother—disagreed. She sat me in her kitchen sink, washed out the wound, and told me that it really didn't hurt that much. I learned then that *dolor* is the pain of the heart in addition to the foot, and my heart did not take well to being called a liar. I also learned that complaining about pain is risky. I became like so many of us who have stories of intense pain, and even know to expect pain from time to time, but don't talk about it nearly enough. Our ideas about *dolor*, like our ideas about anger, are largely brought to us by ancient Greek and Roman philosophers. Blame them if you find our world a bit emotionally anemic.

In ancient Athens, you could always tell who belonged to which philosophical school by where they gathered. Aristotle's "actions-matter-more-than-feelings" students literally followed him around all day and continued walking and talking after he died. The "feelings-can-be-controlled" Stoics met on the front porch of a building that is now in ruins. Epicurus's followers gathered in his garden, tucked away from the bad influence of city life. The setting suited them: flowers of happiness are said to grow out of Epicurean soil.

Epicurus believed that we are unhappy thanks to an always brewing "storm in our soul."[2] He blamed our unhappiness on two factors: first, we fixate on getting things we want, and then, when we get them, we become anxious about losing them. He noticed that a person feeling pain is not feeling pleasure, and that pleasure annoyingly gets ruined by pain. We might be visiting with our elderly mother, listening to her tell the story of her first love, when, out of nowhere, we pick up the smell of death on her breath. We love our partners well and true, until one day we feel the stomach-drop of disappointment. Lucky for us, Epicurus had a cure for "pain from want": stop wanting new stuff, and don't worry about losing your old stuff. This cure, along with the fact that women and slaves were allowed into the garden as a matter of principle, makes Epicureanism quite appealing. Epicurus became a celebrity, almost a god, and then after his death he became a legend.

Early on in the semester, I ask my students: Would you rather be good or happy? The greedy ones go for both: they think a person should be able to be both good and happy. I tell them Aristotle's their man. Others choose good. This group usually has experience with self-sacrifice and reckons that every person must choose whether to be a decent human being or look out for number one. To these students I offer the Stoics, who rank virtue above pleasure. The third group wants to be happy but does not want to look selfish. Luckily, they always have a leader in the back of the classroom who shrugs his shoulders and says, "YOLO."* "The Epicureans are your people," I respond.

Epicurus was a Hedonist, which means that he thought about everything good, even virtue, in terms of pleasure. If we're really being honest, he reasoned, everyone just wants to be happy. Epicurus agreed with the Stoics that happiness meant *ataraxia*—freedom from worry. But he thought it also meant *aponia*—freedom from pain. You cannot be happy if you are miserable, he reasoned. And because pleasure can be fleeting and *dolor* can be relentless, Epicureans try to maximize pleasure and minimize pain.[3] Happiness, for Epicurus, is the opposite of *dolor*.

Hedonism is sometimes criticized for advising us to maximize pleasure. The word "Epicurean" might evoke the image of a rich older man on a couch being fed grapes while getting fanned by a young, half-naked slave waving a giant leaf. The word also gets thrown at Hollywood celebrities who buy a second mansion or an island and tycoons who spend thousands at a restaurant for dinner. Shallow criticisms of the rich and famous often amount to little more than jealousy, but the more incisive critics reject maximizing pleasure as the goal of life.

Unfortunately, neither the spenders nor their critics seem to have studied Epicurus. To the disappointment of my young get-rich-quickers, I announce that the pleasures of the celebrities are not the kinds of pleasures Epicurus had in mind when he equated pleasure with happiness. Real Epicureans don't seek luxuries. They seek pleasures that are small, attainable, and simple. The woman who salivates at 4:00 PM thinking of the rice and beans she plans to eat for dinner will come out happier than

---

*Translation for my friends who have no contact with millennials: "You Only Live Once."

the woman whose palate has gotten accustomed to oysters and Veuve Clicquot but who cannot afford them. If you want only what is within your power to secure, said Epicurus, you will be set for life. Instead of working hard to increase your power and wealth, concentrate on simplifying your desires. Happiness is neither the gambler's high nor the thrill of the chase. It's a stable pleasure that you reach by maximizing the simple pleasures.

But for happiness to remain stable you also need to minimize pain. "Mental suffering," Epicurus admitted, "is agony to endure." But "once you grasp the Epicurean philosophy you won't need to face it again." So don't bother worrying about physical pain, Epicurus reassured us, because it is usually not a problem.* By minimizing mental and emotional pain and embracing a simple and healthy lifestyle, we can free our souls from "disturbance" and begin living a "blessed life."[4]

If Epicureanism sounds reasonable, or at least familiar, it's because we live in a culture that has inherited the idea that pleasure is good and pain is bad. Epicurus's claim that pleasure is an "innate good" and the "starting-point and goal of living blessedly" is hard to deny. Who says no to more pleasure and less pain? We can find updated versions of the Epicurean method and ancient calculus not only in the "Overcoming Negativity" corner of the bookstore but also in the children's section.

A Little Spot of Sadness, published in 2019, bills itself as a book about "empathy and compassion."[5] The dedication tells kids that they have the power to "calm" their "sadness spot" into a "peaceful spot." According to the author, Diane Alber, "we feel the best" when we convert sadness, anxiety, and anger into peace. Crying can help you feel better, she writes. Compassion

---

*Epicurus died a slow and painful death from a kidney stone blocking his urinary tract.

and empathy can calm a friend's "sadness spot," as can love, play, and creativity. Alber ends the book by saying that you can calm your own sadness spot by tracing a circle in the middle of your palm and taking a deep breath.

Alber does not want us to suffer any more than Epicurus did, and she is giving kids tools to minimize their *dolor*. She is genuinely trying to help, and if we're going to remain trapped in the Light Metaphor, in which darkness is best minimized, her tools might help us fit in. Still, when someone offers you "tools," the language suggests that something's broken. What is it exactly that Alber thinks is broken in sad children?

Diane Alber is no psychologist, so we might look to the professionals if we want to know how we should really think about *dolor*. We might expect psychologists to reject a theory that holds that white spots are better than black spots, or that if we want to feel happier we'll need to feel less sad. But positive psychologists turn out to be surprisingly Epicurean.

———

In *The Optimistic Child*—which argues that optimistic kids fare better than pessimistic ones—Martin Seligman tells a story meant to illuminate the perils of pessimism. But I want to convince you that it in fact shows the complex nature of our *dolores*. Jody is a stay-at-home wife and mother whose children have grown up and who is now looking to reenter the workforce. At the dinner table one night, Jody reveals to her husband and teenage son that she is feeling anxious and worried about having been unemployed for almost ten years. But before she can say anything about her feelings, her caring husband reminds her how much she enjoyed her last job as a realtor, so "why don't you start by giving them a call?"[6]

Jody says that she does not want to work for that company again. Her husband changes strategies: maybe they can make a list of her strengths and interests and brainstorm together about jobs that would be a good fit. Just like that, Jody's husband and son are off to the races. They start spitballing about the ways in which being a good mother is surprisingly marketable. They characterize Jody as "patient," "creative," and "full of energy," leading her husband to suggest that she work at one of the "daycare places."[7] It quickly dawns on him, though, that patience, creativity, and energy extend even beyond childcare. Before he can pitch his next idea, Jody gets in a word of protest:

> I appreciate all your help, but I just can't see it happening. No matter what job we come up with, the fact of the matter is that *I will be competing against people a lot younger, who have a lot more education, and who haven't been out of the work force for a decade.* Why hire a middle-aged housewife when you can have someone with better training and better qualifications?[8]

Jody's husband is finding her to be a tough nut to crack: "Boy, Jody, you really are feeling nervous." But he will not be deterred. He cheerfully announces that all Jody needs is a "jump-start."[9] He suggests that she use the week to fix up her résumé and peruse the help-wanted ads. A concrete strategy, for sure. Now Jody's son chimes in, comparing her daunting task to cleaning his room. After all, didn't Mom teach him to pick up all the clothes off the floor before tackling the bookshelves? Jody tries one last time to get through to her husband and son:

> This isn't a matter of me needing a kick to get started. *It's a matter of me not having what it takes to get hired* and no matter

how many cute little gimmicks we try to motivate me, the bottom line is going to stay the bottom line.[10]

Jody's husband and son are working hard to minimize her particular kind of *dolor*, her mix of worry, self-doubt, and whichever unnamed pains lie deeper inside. Jody is hurt, and she is not about to let her family calm her sadness spot. Every time they say, "Oh yes you can!" she says, "I can't." Later that night her son might think of a convincing retort he should have used: *The Little Engine That Could*. Jody probably read it to him when he was small and discouraged, so now all she has to do is read it to herself.

Seligman concludes from Jody's story that she was a "brooding pessimist" who suffered from "catastrophic thoughts." He applauds her family's attempts to "counter her negativity" with positivity. They were right and she was wrong. She had a bad "explanatory style," and they had a better one.[11] In essence, Seligman credits the husband and son with making better arguments than Jody could about her own situation. She was interpreting her circumstances incorrectly and needed some tools to get it right. Jody was in the dark, and her family was lovingly trying to bring her into the light.

There is no underestimating Martin Seligman's professional status and popular reach. Far from a backdoor healer with a crystal and a kooky idea, Seligman is a groundbreaking, award-winning professional psychologist, the founder of "positive psychology," and an expert in clinical depression with decades of experience treating *dolores* like Jody's, that blur the lines between emotional, physical, psychical, and mental pain. One year after the publication of *The Optimistic Child*, he became the president of the American Psychological Association by the largest majority vote in modern history. Seligman has a popular audience, and his (Epicurean) ideas have been accepted and endorsed by experts all over the country.

I'd bet my teeth that other positive psychologists would love to work with Jody, to show her how capable she is and how her negative self-talk is sabotaging her happiness. They are well versed in giving people like Jody tools to change that narrative and go after that job. Give Jody the facts. Pump her with the light of "perspective" until she sees how employable she is. But after pronouncing Jody objectively wrong, Seligman says no more about her. He offers her to readers only as an example of distorted thinking. Perhaps he believes that a middle-aged, out-of-work housewife should have little problem landing a job. *All she has to do is believe in herself and show the world how patient, creative, and energetic she is.* The logic continues: *Jody surely won't be able to pull this off if she's busy brooding.*

Seligman has treated thousands of children and adults in pain. He has seen *dolor* so dark that it becomes numb, as well as despair, hopelessness, and suicides up close. He cares about people no less than Epicurus and Diane Alber, and like his predecessors, Seligman has a light to shine on those of us in the dark.

But is it possible that Seligman's light blinded him from recognizing nyctophobia (fear of the dark) when he saw it? Perhaps Jody's husband and son were so afraid of her darkness that, just as she was inviting them in, they gagged her with solutions. Could Jody have been right to be sad or pessimistic about her job prospects? Could it be that her husband and son were great spitballers but exceptionally bad listeners? Jody was feeling down (which is common enough) and their response was to try to bring her up (also common enough). This countering move is lovingly offered in the name of balance: if someone is having a bad day, balance them out with positivity.

Epicureanism has inspired a whole list of related opposites: pleasure/pain, pessimism/optimism, happiness/sadness. No less than in ancient Greece we're told in America that if we want to be happy, we'll have to stop being so sad. We are told that to defeat *dolor* we should shine some evidence on it, but what about all the evidence of sexist and ageist hiring practices that Jody saw clearly?

It's not the Epicurean idea of maximizing pleasure that has been plaguing our society, but the knee-jerk assumption that sadness is the simple opposite of happiness, that to get happier we need only to cast out sadness. What do we lose by thinking this way? How have we increased suffering by trying to decrease *dolor*?

Let's imaginatively return to Jody's story to see what might come next if we continue to follow in the Epicurean light. After dinner, she considers calling her best friend to talk about the blend of uncomfortable emotions she's dealing with. But Jody doesn't even pick up the phone because she knows what will happen. Her loving friend will tell her the same thing her loving family told her:

"You're going to do great! Stop doubting yourself!"

Anything Jody says at this point will be counted against her as confirmation bias, which happens when people see "only the evidence that confirms their view of themselves and the world" and dismiss evidence to the contrary.[12] Suspecting that her real feelings are making everyone uncomfortable, Jody stifles them.

The next morning at breakfast Jody hides her *dolor* more than usual. She fakes a bright smile when her husband and son ask how she is doing. When they leave the house, though, Jody slumps down at the kitchen table. She still feels sad and worried, but now she also feels alone and ashamed that she cannot muster the confidence they are looking for. *It would make them so happy*, she thinks. *A stronger woman wouldn't be so insecure or hung up by what's starting to smell like a midlife crisis. A better wife and mother wouldn't disappoint her family.* Unfortunately, Jody's shame neither makes her feel better nor increases her job prospects.

Dolor doesn't always get lifted by optimism, but it does get considerably piled on by shame—feeling bad about feeling bad. Anyone who is convinced that happiness can be boot-strapped but who nevertheless experiences sadness must now contend with feelings of weakness or laziness, of not trying hard enough. Cue the Brokenness Story. On top of feeling fear, doubt, and regret, we also now feel shame over disappointing our loved ones, who, as the story goes, *are only trying to help.*

A culture that applauds Jody's husband and son without ever suspecting that they are emotionally shutting her out is a culture that can't handle *dolor*, and in fact, far from handling it, this culture literally drops it. In a world where sad = bad, the sad are doomed. Every time someone says, "Cheer up," "Don't cry," or "I'm sure you'll do fine," they are trying to hand us a flashlight instead of trying to grasp our *dolor*. When platitudes do not pull us out of pain, though, they can plunge us deeper into loneliness. Psychologists who offer tools to the world's Jodys instead of to their loved ones are in danger of missing the forest of societal dysfunction for the tree of *dolor* sitting on their couch. Is there a way to think about *dolor* that does not trigger the Brokenness Story?

———

On my desk you'll find a slip of paper I cut out from a 365-day calendar on how to be happy, like a new kind of fortune cookie that tells you what to do instead of what will happen in your future. Stripped of its date, the note now perpetually advises, "Don't talk about your irritations." I smirk when I picture some stranger sitting at my computer, reading this note, and smiling in approval, imagining me virtuously holding back my complaints for the good of my family, coworkers, society, or even myself. How loving and loved we would be, this advice implies, if we kept our negative feelings to ourselves so as not to burden one another with them. If we spent more time learning to hide, deny, and swallow our irritations, surely we would be happier.

If the Spanish philosopher Miguel de Unamuno heard this, or had read Jody's story, he would shout in protest. He would urge us to see Jody as a woman of *carne y hueso* (flesh and bone) who, in expressing her *dolor*, was bravely asking to be seen by her family. As a person fluent in fourteen languages, Unamuno cared a great deal about communication. He might even go as far as to pronounce Jody's family emotionally illiterate.

Born in 1864 in Bilbao, Miguel de Unamuno was the fruit of incest. His father Félix was forty when he married his niece, Salomé. Félix had recently returned to Spain after living and working in Mexico. Salomé and Félix had six children, and Miguelito, the future patron saint of melancholy, was one of only four who survived their genetic disadvantage.

Félix died from tuberculosis before his little boy turned six. Miguelito remembered little about him, and on the surface, the old man's death does not seem to have affected him. It's hard to believe, though, that losing a father at such a tender age did not contribute to Unamuno's adult preoccupation with pain, suffering, and death. *Dolor* colors all of Unamuno's philosophy, and his 1913 book *The Tragic Sense of Life* can be read as changing

Descartes's 1637 philosophical dictum "I think therefore I am" into "I suffer, therefore I am."[13]

Unamuno married his childhood sweetheart Concha, and together they had nine children. Blue-eyed Raimundo, the sixth child, developed hydrocephalus (a buildup of fluid in the cavities deep within the brain) and died of meningitis when he was six, the same age Miguelito had been when his father died. Unamuno's Catholic faith temporarily collapsed under the weight of Raimundo's prolonged illness and death. The bereaved father's life became a "constant meditation on death."[14]

Unamuno tried to write as contrarily as he could. "The greatest part of my work," he admitted, "has been to disquiet my neighbors, to stir up the sediment of their hearts, to sow anguish in them, if possible."[15] Here's one dramatic attempt:

> Reader, listen. Though I do not know you, I love you so much that if I could hold you in my hands, I would open up your breast and in your heart's core I would make a wound and into it I would rub vinegar and salt, so that you might never again know peace but would live in continual anguish and endless longing.[16]

Unamuno loves us no less than Epicurus, Diane Alber, and Martin Seligman do. But unlike them, he doesn't want to fix our *dolor*. Living free from pain, says Unamuno, does not make for a meaningful life. He desperately wants us to dig up the living and dying, the pain and suffering and longing we have stored inside of us next to our "arsenal of anger."[17] Unamuno's most philosophical book, *The Tragic Sense of Life*, was his attempt to agitate the Spanish people into waking up from their slumber, as Socrates had tried to do for the Athenians. Both philosophers tried to wake people up in the name of love.

A word of warning: Unamuno's philosophy is somewhat extreme. It is a tougher sell than emotional tranquility, and it can be dangerous for masochists. Unamuno did not want us to court *dolor*, but he insisted that we not ignore it as it arrives in our lives daily, weekly, monthly, yearly. We need not invite suffering. And we need never thank it for coming. But we can receive it when it shows up on our doorstep, and it will.

When Unamuno and Concha lost their blue-eyed baby, they shared a *dolor* that few couples know and even fewer survive. Unamuno called it an "embrace of despair" that led to the birth of "true spiritual love." Although he had loved Concha since he was fourteen, and although their bodies had merged in the marriage bed, he reports that their souls didn't merge "until the heavy pestle of sorrow bruised their hearts and crushed them in the same mortar of suffering."[18] Together, Unamuno says, he and Concha bowed beneath the "yoke of a common grief," and it opened a new dimension to their marriage. He found out that *dolor* offers more than just hurt.

Unamuno's famous phrase "the tragic sense of life" refers to the fact that every living thing dies. When someone we care deeply about dies, we are left in ruins, with bloodshot eyes that see *dolor* everywhere. Our choice is then either to minimize darkness or to sit with it. Epicureans would advise the first. But what about the second option? If we sit with *dolor*, will we get stuck there?

Eventually, we must each adopt a stance toward the darker side of our emotional life. The Epicureans offer one philosophy of *dolor*—happiness and sadness cannot coexist—which, I've suggested, leads to shame. Unamuno offers an alternative philosophy that can help us live with *dolor* and better understand it as an essential part of our shared human condition as creatures who suffer and die.

In the United States, advice like my calendar's ("don't talk about your irritations") is standard. Expressing your irritations—announcing what's causing you pain, sadness, discomfort—makes people cringe. *Dolor* is hard to hear. But sadly, we too often get the message that, if you really love your family, hide your darkest thoughts and feelings from them. They cannot bear to see you sad, and it will make them sad. Worse, it will make them feel helpless.

If Unamuno had made a calendar, the quote from him that I would unironically cut out for display would read: "Whenever I have felt a pain I have shouted and I have done it publicly."[19] He believed that expressing *dolor* should be seen as a gift to the people around you, as an act of handing them a string like the one Ariadne gave to the Greek hero Theseus when he entered Centaur's labyrinth. Ariadne's string led Theseus out of the labyrinth, but ours leads our loved ones into the maze where we feel alone with our *dolor*. To an Epicurean-leaning society, though, the suggestion that divulging your *dolor* constitutes a gift to your loved ones sounds backwards, countercultural, obscene even. My sister used to eat the slobbered-on Cheerios her baby offered her as a gift. Maybe Unamuno's idea sounds a little like that.

Jody's family's failure to see her expression of *dolor* as a gift deprived them of a connection with a woman who seldom talked about her feelings. In trying to help her, they overlooked her. Like a dog who had been reprimanded, Jody's *dolor* responded by slinking away. Many of us are like Jody, and although we might like to believe Brené Brown that vulnerability is strength, our comforters keep getting frustrated and dropping our strings. They are stuck in the Light Metaphor, asking, *What can I do? How can I fix it?* So they leave us alone in the dark where the temptation to tell ourselves the Brokenness Story is unrelenting.

Unamuno did not consider *dolor* the opposite of happiness, and he certainly did not feel compelled to minimize it. He believed that countering negativity with positivity cuts off opportunities for intimacy and connection, for empathy and compassion. If Unamuno were alive today, he would advise us to fight the "tyranny of the positive attitude," knowing that doing so would earn us puzzled looks from people who cheerfully say: "You get what you get and you don't get upset."[20] But in doing so we would be joining those who believe that negativity is neither broken nor useless and that pain, sorrow, and loss make us human. You get what you get and sometimes it's upsetting.

Why talk about your irritations? To give people in your life a chance to love you. Sorrow craves acknowledgment and expression, not repression or cheering up. Pain is a sign of vitality, and acknowledging it gives us eyes to recognize it when it's sitting across the kitchen table. People in pain are not broken. They're just in pain.

More suffering would come for Unamuno after the death of his son, and with it, more fodder for his philosophy of suffering. In 1924 he was removed from his position as rector of the University of Salamanca and exiled by the Spanish government to the island of Fuerteventura because he was an outspoken intellectual who refused to bow to dictators. After six months he escaped to France, where he stubbornly lived for six years in protest against Primo de Rivera's regime. Unamuno came home after Rivera's death only to stir up more political trouble. At an event where Unamuno presided as the reinstated rector, a high-ranking Francoist shouted the slogan "Death to intelligence! Long live death!" Instead of keeping his mouth shut, Unamuno yelled back.[21] This time, instead of exiling him, they put him under house arrest.

Unamuno did not survive his punishment, nor did he get to see the end of the Spanish Civil War. Some say he was murdered for his outspoken opposition to Franco's government, and some say he died of natural causes. Unamuno was seventy-two and adored by a people to whom he had offered a tragic and poetic identity. His popular writings had praised Spain's fine literature, poetry, music, and art, and he had wanted his fellow Spaniards to recover their artistic and literary souls—including, of course, an aesthetic appreciation of *dolor*.

Unamuno's philosophy spread to Latin America and even the Peale-riddled United States in the decades that followed. His meditations on *dolor* caught on among readers who were rebelling against *The Power of Positive Thinking*. From the 1960s to the 1980s, Unamuno's books were taught in philosophy classes, where meditating on death was par for the course. Unfortunately, Unamuno became a casualty of the light. As we have grown more and more nyctophobic in the United States, Unamuno's ideas have fallen away. When I mention teaching him in the presence of college-educated people in their sixties, they smile widely and tell me they read him in philosophy class. It's rare to have that experience with anyone in their thirties.

Unamuno believed that *dolor* wants to be acknowledged, not ignored or lectured at. But our expressions of *dolor* are often mishandled, as in Jody's case. Our comforters do not realize that an expression of *dolor* is meant to trigger compassion and connection, not dismissive solutions.

We do not have to lose a child, as Unamuno did, to know emotional pain, but we do have to sometimes feel *dolor*. We can't always just trace circles on our hands until it goes away. *Dolor* may visit unannounced, but ignoring the doorbell does not mean it isn't waiting there on the doorstep. A world without *dolor* would certainly be a brighter world, but a brighter world would likely be an emotionally emaciated one. If we mistakenly interpret *dolor* as a synonym for "something's wrong with me," we will overlook the element of compassion, both for ourselves and for others. Like Theseus making his way out of a dark and confusing labyrinth because he held on to the string given to him in love by Ariadne, we must hang on to the string given to us by someone we love that will lead us into the maze of their *dolor*.

Once we grow in compassion for our fellow sufferers, Unamuno says, the chain of compassion keeps expanding. Love "personalizes" everything that it has compassion for, he notes, including trees, animals, insects. In the other's *dolor* I recognize that we are the same. Unamuno writes:

> We love only that which is like us and thus our compassion grows, and with it our love for things in the measure to which they are discovered to be in our likeness. If I am moved to pity and love the luckless star which will one day vanish from the sky, it is because love, compassion, makes me feel that it possesses a consciousness, more or less obscure, which causes it to suffer because it is no more than a star doomed to cease being itself one day.[22]

When we respond to someone's *dolor*, we grow in compassion and love for them.[23] This kind of love—Unamuno calls it "spiritual"—is born of tragedy, and it sometimes leads us back to a self we have been estranged from. *Dolor* can open our eyes to what we had not previously seen.

In failing to accept Jody's gift, her husband and son failed to locate her. She was reaching for them (in words no less, which is something of a miracle), but their assumptions about *dolor* prevented them from inching closer to her. Focused on combat instead of compassion, they could not find her. She had handed them a string, but they dropped it. Their hands were full of flashlights.

Maybe Jody's family minimized her *dolor* because they believed that we grow more intimate with one another when we are up than when we are down. Maybe her husband imagined the celebratory dinner they would eat on Jody's first day at her new job. They would be so proud, and she would be so proud, and that idyllic night would be the right time for connecting on a deep level. They would keep the lights on.

But do humans connect best when their spirits are up? Epicurus probably believed that, and so might Diane Alber and Martin Seligman. Unamuno admitted it is true for bodies, which unite in "supreme delight." It is not true for souls, though, he thought. Our spirits connect better through *dolor*.[24] Support groups are formed to share sorrow, and that is where people often feel most seen. *Dolor* draws people into the same "mortar of suffering" and gives us a chance to see one another in the dark.

Although Jody's husband wanted to inspire her with his positive attitude, he couldn't. This is bright-sidedness's downfall: upbeat feelings can blind people to suffering. Either because they don't want to or, as is often the case, they just can't, upbeat people do not see that they can make things worse with their positivity. It takes serious effort for someone we love to keep themselves tender-hearted enough to hold our pain, especially when they are not in pain. It is much easier for them to suppress, deny, and reject our *dolor*, and our society will applaud them for doing so. Inside the Light Metaphor, our suffering is a hindrance to others' joy.

Given our Epicurean-leaning society, it is truly tragic that *dolor* sees better in the dark than joy does. *Dolor* can spot a fellow sufferer even if she's got a tan and a new pair of jeans.[25] *Dolor* sees her as a "companion in misery" underneath the shiny new facade, to borrow a phrase from the philosopher Arthur Schopenhauer. People unattuned to *dolor* see only the externals and assume that our sufferer is healthy and happy. But just as is true in the physical world, we are better equipped to see someone in the dark if our eyes have already adjusted. Our ability to see suffering people (which the self-help industry might, in time, come to call a superpower) depends on our willingness to lovingly confront our own suffering without automatically concluding that we or other sufferers are broken. *Dolor* is a radar we cannot manufacture, but it's also one that all of us already have the parts for and, with patient practice, can build.

It's important to be honest about how we feel, but it's also important to look around. If we are stifling, ignoring, or trying to minimize our *dolor*, we are probably missing the suffering of people like us. If Jody's husband had been experiencing a midlife crisis, he might have seen her better. He might have observed: *You are like me.* That realization might have led them to some radically honest conversations. They might have learned about her ambivalence over the past ten years. "I've lost time," she might say, "I've lost credibility." Maybe she was afraid that CEOs and coworkers would see her as a housewife, not as a capable individual. "It's not fair," she might add, "that the workforce looks down on older women. This society is rough on people over fifty trying to make a career for themselves." If her husband and son had been receptive, Jody might even have expressed her unfulfilled wish to have been a full-time mother while staying employed full-time. She had not wanted to miss out on her kid's childhood, she would say, but neither had she wanted to quit work.

"In this country," she might add, "they make you choose. And now I have to pay for the choice I made. No matter how creative and patient I am, and even if I had as much energy as you seem to think I have, I'm not as competitive as a thirty-year-old. I don't regret staying home, but I grieve my professional self these last ten years." That night at the dinner table, Jody might have become a whole human being for her family instead of remaining just "wife" and "mother." If only they had dimmed the lights.

Doubts do not vanish because someone tells you not to worry, but they might loosen their grip if you sense the other person is not out to minimize them. If Jody's family were to continue having "heart-to-hearts" like this hypothetical one, they would draw closer. Jody would trust that she did not have to hide her worries or put on a "brave" face for their sake. She would be convinced that they could handle her sadness, doubts, and frustrations. She would know that she need not face her *dolor* alone. Her husband and son, likewise, would feel safer being more vulnerable with each other and with Jody. Who knows what kinds of conversations could flow between us if we could stop stifling our *dolor* and instead start talking about it regularly?

Unamuno's endorsement of the bonding quality of *dolor* suggests that we think of it less as a toxin we brew and poison each other with, and more as a cup of sorrow provided by nature that we pass around and sometimes drink from together. We can take from Unamuno a resolve to stop combating *dolor*. When we find ourselves in a dolorous mood, we can look around and respond to other people's bids for compassion. In those times, we can practice receiving a string and holding on to it. Preceding Brené Brown by a hundred years, Unamuno's penchant for vocalizing his *dolor* suggests that he would agree with her currently popular idea that it requires strength, not weakness, to be vulnerable. If Unamuno is right that authentic love can be found by sharing the cries of our heart with one another, we can look at moments of shared pain as pathways to connection.

I may be the only one of my siblings who wants to see my father get sicker. For a year now, he's been healing from a stroke he suffered on the heels of a heart attack. My father had never been a stranger to physical pain—I had heard that as a young man he fractured his arm and did not go to the doctor, and that another time he broke an ankle ice skating but waited out a two-day snowstorm in the Bronx to get to the emergency room. Lots of physicians like my father are reluctant to go to the hospital because they see the examining table from the other side. As a pathologist, my father's examining table was located in the morgue. In the forty years I knew him before his stroke, I never heard him complain about physical pain or mental suffering.

In the ICU at eighty-five, my father experienced *dolor*. He grimaced through IV needle insertions and blood draws. Although he was closer than ever to death, I had never seen him more human and alive. I had considered my father pain-resistant to a fault, so I had never felt comfortable talking to him about my own pain. I made other connections with him instead, including our mutual love of literature and poetry. Our relationship got smoother as he got older and his temper died down, but I had never seen my father vulnerable until he shared his *dolor*.

In the hospital, my father went through a lot of darkness concerning his past and experienced some guilt and paranoia. That is apparently normal for his type of stroke. It was sad to watch but also exhilarating. I had never seen so much emotion coming from him—no, better put: I had never seen so much emotion coming from him that wasn't anger.

On his worst day during my visit, my father's potassium level dropped dangerously low. The doctors had tried oral potassium, but it was not working, so they decided on an IV. Since he had refused intubation, owing to his advanced age, the only portal was through his arm, which, according to the internet, is a dreadful place to inject potassium because of the sting. I read reports of grown men having to stop their infusion because the pain was so severe. Potassium chloride, I also learned, is one of the chemicals mixed into a lethal injection. When the drip started, my father cried out and didn't stop. "*¡No me abusen! ¡Sean buenas conmigo! ¡Por favor!*" (Don't abuse me! Be good to me! Please!) I was gutted, but everyone around me seemed to be acting as though he were a big baby. I could tell that my father was feeling pain and was shouting it publicly. Like Unamuno, he was humanized by his suffering, and I was grateful. He was finally teaching me how and when to cry out. Unamuno publicized the cries of his heart "to make the heart-strings of others vibrate."[26] The grieving chords of my father's heartstrings got mine vibrating, and I was able to draw close to him in a new way for a time. Without his cries, I would not have known him. Crying out publicly does not guarantee closeness, but it can foster it. Jody cried out, but no one heard. What if they had?

In the hospital elevator, I asked a man in scrubs how he could work there amid so much pain. I had just witnessed a woman and man embracing and crying tenderly in the hallway. He said that he saw the opposite: joy and hope even in the sickest of patients. I wondered if this man's experience would challenge my Unamunian theory about *dolor*, compassion, and connection. But then I realized that the acceptance of illness puts people in a position to share an "embrace of despair." Joy and hope need not be bright-sided. Maybe what that man in scrubs sometimes witnessed was not the denial of suffering and death but the joy and hope of renewed or strengthened relationships. Physical and psychic pain may rub us red and raw, but once our skin is off, we become sensitive to the pain of others. Sadness is not the opposite of happiness.

Home and healing four months later, my father became quiet again, reserved, more lucid. He didn't want to hold my hand anymore or lie in bed and have me read him poems. As he began getting fully dressed and groomed each day, he moved farther away from me. We still have good days, but as he regains his sense of shame, his vulnerability disappears.

What kind of sadistic daughter must I be, to wish my father ill? But I don't. I want to hold his hand, and unfortunately this can happen only when he's ill. I found joy and connection—a different kind of healing—during the most vulnerable parts of my father's illness. Now, as he experiences "healing," as traditionally defined, he is becoming once again a man who doesn't talk about his *dolor*. He reaches for me—for tender human connection—only when he is sick. Illness is not required for connection, of course, but vulnerability is—the vulnerability that hides from the light and emerges in the dark. It would be better, of course, if we could manage to shed some layers before having a brush with death. But it's hard to do in a world where happiness calendars instruct us not to talk about our irritations. Deathbed reunions and reconciliations come, if at all, after decades of stifled regrets, stiff upper lips, and silenced *dolores*.

Seen through Unamuno's lens, *dolor* isn't a sign of brokenness. It is an agitation that can lead us to call out to our loved ones. But they don't always hear our call. Sorrow *can* make us more accessible to each other, but nowhere does Unamuno say it must. Instead, he asks why connection does not always happen. His answer is harsh: it's no use "if [others] don't have heartstrings, [or] if they are so rigid that they won't vibrate," he spits out. "My cry will not resonate in them."[27]

I like to think that our loved ones have heartstrings, but that some have grown rigid after years of being taught to ignore pain and calm sadness spots. We have been given crummy advice with the best of intentions, and our emotional lives have suffered.

Most of us are still new at seeing in the dark, even if we have been living in the dark for a while, but philosophers like Unamuno can help. His *dolor* asks if our heartstrings have grown rigid and teaches us that love consists in listening without bailing or pep talks. Emotional pain can lower our defenses and make us emotionally honest, perhaps to a degree we have never been before.

What wisdom could Jody's family or even Seligman take away from Unamuno? If Unamuno had been able to decide how Jody's family would react to her *dolor* that evening at the dining room table, it might have gone like this. Jody expresses her doubts and worries about being able to find a good job at her age. Her husband and son, denying their knee-jerk, self-protective impulse to shine a light on Jody's darkness, turn toward her and lean in. They ask nonrhetorical questions, and they listen as if her words are sacred. As the three of them sit in the dark, Jody's husband and son begin to pay attention. They ask her what she's most worried about: "Is it managing the work hours, doubts about your competence, or feelings about having a boss?"

In the cave there's a lot of silence, the silence of listening, feeling, and thinking. They give Jody enough space to think out loud, even talk in circles if that helps her acclimate to being in the dark and figure out what she feels. It's more than low self-regard, she discovers. As her husband and son listen, they learn what a lot of intelligent older women have already learned: ten years at home puts a housewife looking for work at a disadvantage. Jody's not wrong. She's not a brooding pessimist. Her feelings make sense. Then something magical happens: her husband's and son's heartstrings begin vibrating. What they are hearing from Jody moves them, and her husband takes her hand. He asks if she feels left behind, too old, or no longer capable. All three hearts move in concert:

"It must have been hard to swap career-casual for spit-up rags."

They go deeper.

"Do you wish you hadn't stopped working?"

Sensing that she's in a different space now, Jody voices her ambivalence without fear of offending them.

"No. I would do it again. But I wish I could have had both a successful career and have been the kind of mother I wanted to be. I wouldn't take back those years, but they do represent a loss for me, and not just in the eyes of other people. Sometimes I wish we lived in Denmark or Sweden where they help you have both. It just doesn't feel fair that I had to choose, and now I am paying for that choice."

"Yes," say her husband and son, their emotional IQ rising by the minute. Jody's family learns that you don't need to take away a person's *dolor* to give them the joy of compassion. The Epicureans were wrong: we can feel good and bad together. It can feel good to know that our loved ones won't run away when we feel bad.

Heartstrings in harmony say yes instead of no. They vibrate based on connection. When her family is done with sitting, listening, and affirming, Jody feels closer to them, better understood, and validated. She has spoken her *dolor*, and no one chased it back down her throat. Now that Jody's *dolor* has been heard instead of castigated, she can unclench her fists and entertain the possibility that she might get a job. Talking through her *dolor* might even have given her an idea of what field she would like to pursue as a more mature woman. Jody goes to bed that night feeling loose, flexible, relaxed. She's grateful that her family put down the flashlights and held on to her string. Tonight they saw each other in the dark.

A friend of mine once saw her five-year-old son tracing sad faces on his pillow. She was shattered. She felt guilty and overwhelmed at the straightforwardness of his message. His *dolor* was an indictment of her parenting, his pillow evidence of her failure to keep him happy. My friend thought it too tragic to ask her son about his sad faces, so she pretended not to see them.

Ignoring *dolor* is a common enough move, but what if my friend had taken the string her son was so trustingly offering? She might have come closer to seeing him in the dark if she had simply said:

"It looks like you're sad."

Huddling together in the dark is a good start to gaining night vision. To master it, though, we have to believe that *dolor* looks like failure only in the light. In the dark it looks like heartstrings and spiritual connection.

When we deny, hide, or minimize *dolor*, we do not give people a chance to make their way toward us. Worse, we become clumsy and awkward. We must develop night vision not only for ourselves, but for others. If we want our kids, partners, and friends to talk about their *dolor*, we need to be willing to dim the lights and let our eyes adjust.

And nowhere do we need better night vision than when we grieve—the *dolor* of the living in the face of death.

chapter 3

grieving stubbornly

I once overheard a friend telling a brand-new widower: "I'm so impressed that you're handling this so well." Here was a man, four days out from losing his wife, putting his emotions to work the only way he knew how: by washing dishes and taking care of logistics. "It's great that you're staying busy and keeping it together." I cannot say whether my friend's comments made the widower feel better or worse. Maybe he felt seen, as though his efforts were not a waste of time or energy. Maybe he valued his productivity and was grateful that he did not lose his functioning capacity in addition to his wife. Maybe he liked getting a gold star for grieving well. Or maybe he felt pressure to keep it up.

Later, I asked my friend whether he would be equally impressed if the widower did nothing all day but cry. What if he skipped the dishes and ate Domino's out of the box every night? What if he slept in his wife's robe—and walked around in it all day too? What if he kept the blinds shut and refused phone calls? As far as grief-responses go, is not washing dishes when your wife dies as impressive a way to grieve as washing them?

The kind of person who would support a widower's right to fall apart probably does not use the term "falling apart"—or the term "keeping it together," for that matter. They probably do not describe any grieving style as "impressive." I don't know how many of these emotional rebels exist in the United States, the land where the spring-cleaning style of grief impresses friends and family more than the tragic style, which tends to make people whisper about mental health. Why are nongrievers so determined to keep grievers busy?

My friend was not trying to imply that falling apart would constitute a bad grief response. He was genuinely shocked by how "well" the widower was doing with the business of grieving a death, and he confessed that he didn't know if he would be that "strong." In a world where the Light Metaphor declares that staying busy is impressive, the Brokenness Story wastes no time in informing unproductive grievers that they are deficient. They will receive (and likely internalize) the societal message that they are succumbing to their grief instead of mastering it. They are doing grief wrong.

Both my friend and the widower were raised to believe that strength means toughing it out. They, along with millions of us across multiple generations, were taught that it is healthier to keep active than to let yourself collapse from grief. Leeat Granek is a social scientist who calls this attitude, when taken by doctors, a "pathologization of grief." Too often when it comes to treating grief, "the goal is to get people functioning and back to work in a timely and cost-efficient manner."[1] Insurance companies certainly prefer treatments that have an end date. A person who mourns quickly and cleanly will be deemed healthier and more successful than a person who doesn't. But is keeping busy the only legitimate way of grieving? Must everyone wash dishes?

Megan Devine, a grief expert from whom we will hear later, was told in her grief that what she really needed was to go dancing. It was days after her partner drowned. Here was the Light Metaphor strong-arming her to stay on the sunny side of life. Here too was the Brokenness Story, ready to attack if she refused. She didn't wash their sheets for a year, and as we'll see in a bit, she defends every minute of her grief.

I am terrified to face true grief for the first time, but not because of the *dolor* that death provokes. I'm terrified because, when my time comes, I imagine I will end up on the floor instead of in front of a sink, and I have heard and read too many grief-shaming stories to trust that it will go well. Our society is too entrenched in an emotionally stifling philosophy of grief, and anyone making room for the falling-apart kind— the "wintering" kind, to borrow a term from contemporary author Katherine May—is going to have a tough time.[2]

As with anger and the tangled forms of *dolor* that we examined in the last chapter, the lights of ancient Greek and Roman philosophy are one reason why we rush grieving people through their grieving today. The Roman Stoic Seneca, who praised Plato for castigating his anger, would have been impressed with a widower who keeps busy. In AD 40, Seneca advised his friend Marcia to stop grieving for her dead son. It had been three years, and Seneca had decided to write her a public letter comparing her to two other mothers who had lost their sons. The first, he said, "became the intimate of darkness and solitude," while the second "laid aside her sorrow together with her son" and "grieved no more than was honourable."[3] Seneca was not trying to be a dick when he suggested that Marcia be like the second mother. He genuinely did not want to see his friend in pain, but he also thought her grief was irrational. Marcia was choosing to feel bad, Seneca concluded, and it baffled him: Who would want to grieve for three years?

In the Stoic philosophy, we choose anger, we choose sadness, we choose grief. Feelings don't arise unbidden in the soul, as Aristotle had claimed. Therefore, we should not choose to feel pain. Seneca even compared Marcia's grief to a vice, an "unhealthy pleasure" that trapped her into a bizarre loyalty to suffering. If you asked Seneca, it was Marcia's love of *dolor*, not love of her son, that darkened her grief.

Seneca was convinced that, by this point, Marcia's grief had outlasted her feelings. He asked her to pay attention to how her "sorrow renews itself and takes fresh strength every day."[4] And he suggested that she follow the example of animals, who don't "nourish" their grief.[5] Here was Marcia, picking daily at the scab of grief until it bled, and here was Seneca, furiously trying to cover her hands with mittens.

Seneca's views about dark feelings might sound judgmental, but if Marcia were alive today, it would not be so odd for her friends or mental health professionals to conclude that she was clinging to her grief. Three years is a long time to mourn a loved one. We would hate to see someone caught in that nasty middle that Marcia was caught in, "unwilling to live but unable to die."[6] And we might conclude that her grief was a stand-in for the child she lost—to be held tight and coddled, not forgotten or rejected. We might feel sorry that her life had been reduced so severely, and we might wish her all the happiness in the world. In our particular cultural light, happiness would mean letting go of her son.

In grieving, Seneca says that we cry as much for ourselves and our misuse of time as for our loved ones. We regret having failed to appreciate them while they were alive. If only we could have realized that our loved ones are made of the same gooey mush as we are, that they are subject to the rules of mortality as we are, then our grief would be better, shorter-lived. Since we know people die, Seneca's reasoning goes, why be shocked when they do? Why not prepare? He would not be surprised that some of the young mothers in my classroom have not drawn up a last will and testament. Reading Seneca makes them feel castigated, but they usually think he's right.

It was not only Marcia that Seneca tried to help. He wrote a conciliatory letter to his own mother, who was grieving over him even while he was still alive. (Seneca was exiled after the Roman emperor Caligula accused him of sleeping with his sister.) Seneca also wrote to a man grieving his brother's death. In those two letters, he employed a sequence of arguments similar to those he used with Marcia. The message was always the same: "All life is worthy of our tears: fresh problems will press upon you before you have done with the old ones."[7] His arguments amounted to: *The dead don't feel anything. They don't want your pity. A longer life isn't necessarily a better one. Your grief won't bring them back.* To his mother he added that it could be worse: he could be dead (in which case, presumably, see the letter to Marcia). At the end of all of his consolation letters, Seneca prescribed a remedy: read philosophy and poetry.

Seneca admitted that his method was violent. He opted to "do battle with" and "shatter" grief in order to "conquer" it.[8] He employed "no gentle path to working a remedy, but that of cautery and the knife."[9] It was the only way he could imagine for helping sufferers get past their grief. But then Seneca also tried a softer touch. He reminded Marcia that we are all born to suffer:

To this end you were born, to experience loss and to perish, to feel hope and fear, to disturb others and yourself, to dread and yet to long for death, and, worst of all, never to know under what terms you exist.[10]

If life is painful enough as it is, he reasoned, why would any of us choose to grieve on top of it all? Seneca left no stone unturned. He really wanted people to find *ataraxia*—freedom from worry—and yet he witnessed human beings who, over and over again, chose grief.

Remarkably, Seneca was one of the more lenient Stoics when it came to grief. He allowed people to cry—quickly, though, so they could get back to life, and only if strictly necessary. He was not fond of weeping, but he admitted that it would be "inhuman hardness not to grieve at all."[11] Unlike the stricter Stoics, Seneca permitted grief in moderation, and he defended himself from charges of acerbity by asserting that he would not dry a mother's tears on the day of her child's funeral.[12] (He made no promises about the next day.)

Sixty years before Seneca was born, the Roman statesman and sometime-Stoic Cicero had shamed grievers using what today we'd surely call "toxic masculinity." For instance, he called grief "weak and womanly."[13] And voluntary. To prove that grief is voluntary, Cicero pointed to the many aristocrats and military commanders who stopped their tears from flowing so they wouldn't look "unmanly."[14] *See?* he reasoned. *Grief is not a spontaneous occurrence. You can choose not to.*

To save yourself a "weak and womanly" grief spell, the Stoics suggested practicing *memento mori*: remembering, daily, that you will cease to exist, and also imagining your loved ones as though they were already deceased. This practice should spark gratitude in you while you are still alive. The Stoics are responsible for the old adage that we should embrace those we care about today because we might not have them tomorrow.

When I was practicing Stoicism as a new mother, I daily engaged in *memento mori*, just in case. The Stoics thought that if we meditate on death every single day, we are more likely to appreciate people while they are still alive. *I am going to die*, I would think to myself. *My parents are going to die. My partner is going to die.* I would hold my baby's tiny hand, look at him lovingly as he nursed on my breast, and whisper: *You are going to die.* My students laugh nervously when I admit this, and while I am not overly superstitious, the ritual did make me sweat.

If Seneca was the sweet one, the Southern gentleman of the Stoic bunch, then his successor Epictetus was the straight shooter who lacked a soft spot for our feelings. "If you are fond of a jug," he said, "say you are fond of a jug; then you will not be disturbed if it be broken."[15] By extension, "if you kiss your child or your wife, say to yourself that you are kissing a human being, for then if death strikes it you will not be disturbed."[16]

Maybe Epictetus was this blunt because he had been a slave. Legend has it that his master was twisting his leg as a punishment for something he had done. Smiling, Epictetus said, "You will break my leg." His master kept twisting, and the leg broke. Epictetus asked calmly, "Did I not tell you that you would break it?"[17]

As a New Yorker, I loved Epictetus. He told it straight. I learned from him that pretending my baby was immortal wasn't just idiocy but part of a larger formula for living badly. And it was sure to end in grief if my baby died. The Stoics wanted so badly to help us withstand what Seneca called the "storm" of life (the external version of the storm Epicurus told us we brew in our souls).[18] They argued that if we screw our heads on tightly enough, we will be tranquil and resilient when we capsize and can immediately set about fixing the boat. Expect your wife to die; then you will not stop washing the dishes when she does.

Although I've seen my students perk up at the idea given to us by the Stoics that we control our feelings, and although much of what they say can help us get along in a broken society, the light coming off their training in grief is blinding. However taken I (still) am with the Stoics (for their acknowledgment that life is brutal), I doubt that Seneca's letters brought the grieving recipients much consolation. I cannot agree that grief should be somewhere between nonexistent and swift. Seneca's letters may even have made grievers like Marcia feel worse by publicly shaming them. Grieving is a personal thing, and when death takes a loved one away from me, I will not aim to be tranquil and resilient. I see no virtue in washing dishes. I don't need to impress anyone. Instead, I want the freedom to capsize without apology. Like Montaigne.

On August 17, 1563, Michel de Montaigne sat up all night watching his best friend Étienne de La Boétie die of the plague. Montaigne was thirty years old, and the plague was spreading throughout the south of France. Still, he stayed and risked death for love of his friend. Seventeen years later, Montaigne wrote: "Since that day when I lost him, I merely drag wearily on."[19]

Almost immediately upon meeting La Boétie, Montaigne considered him his other half. Their friendship lasted four years—the best four years of Montaigne's life.[20] After La Boétie's death, Montaigne went on to marry and have children, but no one would ever get as close to him as his friend had. When asked to explain his rare friendship (which more than one gossip had speculated was more than platonic) and just what it was about La Boétie that was so irreplaceable, Montaigne fell short. "If you press me to say why I loved him," he admitted, "I feel that it cannot be expressed except by replying: 'Because it was him: because it was me.'"[21] Montaigne had met his match, and he could not render the experience in words.

Montaigne's grief was chronic. Almost twenty years after La Boétie died, Montaigne still lamented outliving his friend. "In everything we were halves: I feel I am stealing his share from him." Montaigne became one of the most famous essayists in history, but he would forever feel that his life counted for "no more than a half."[22] The ever-grieving friend found solace in the Roman poet Horace:

> Since an untimely blow has borne away a part of my soul, why do I still linger on less dear, only partly surviving? That day was the downfall of us both.[23]

Montaigne was not infected by plague that night, but La Boé-tie's death emptied him. In addition to the people Montaigne found to love in the last twenty-nine years of his life, he carried La Boétie with him unapologetically, refusing to abandon his grief.

In defense of his perennial grief, Montaigne also quoted the Latin poet Catullus: "What shame or limit should there be to grief for one so dear?"[24] This question comes at grief from a darker ethos: *Why be ashamed?* Montaigne's essays are astonishingly vulnerable and personal; for instance, in one of them he tells us which foods make him fart. His essays celebrate the human condition instead of hiding it. Montaigne's love for his friend (at the risk of gossip) and steadfast grief for him for several decades are both examples of dignity. Unapologetic about loving and grieving deeply, Montaigne showed us a decidedly un-Stoic way of being fully human. I think it's beautiful.

But by today's standard, Montaigne's grief would be considered pathological.

Even if Seneca had known that chimpanzees have been known to carry around their dead babies, he probably would not have changed his stance about whether grief is a rational response to loss.[25] The central assumption of Stoicism—that dark moods are avoidable—is one of the lights that trigger contemporary diagnoses of a variety of mental illnesses, including anxiety, depression, and, in the last ten years, grief. Seneca's letters, Epictetus's advice based on the similarities between clay jugs and babies, and Cicero's observation that military commanders can close their mouths and hold back tears laid the ancient foundation for the contemporary light of psychiatry to classify grief as a mental disorder.

"Persistent complex bereavement disorder" used to be called "complicated grief disorder" and is still sometimes colloquially referred to as "complicated grief." It appears between "depressive episodes with short-duration hypomania" and "caffeine use disorder" in the "Conditions for Further Study" section of the fifth edition of the *Diagnostic and Statistical Manual of Mental Disorders* (*DSM-5*).[26] The authors note that none of the conditions that appear in this section are officially recognized and so must not be used for clinical purposes; as such, complicated grief is an unofficial diagnosis, but a diagnosis nevertheless.[27] Less than 5 percent of the US population reportedly suffers from complicated grief. Like anxiety and depression, it is also experienced more by women than men. Apparently, Cicero was right: grief *is* girly.

To qualify for persistent complex bereavement disorder, the grief-stricken must have been mourning the death for at least twelve months and must have experienced one of the following "more often than not": (1) persistent yearning/longing for the deceased, (2) intense sorrow and emotional pain, and (3) preoccupation with either the deceased or the manner of their death. It's not hard to imagine someone having all three of these feelings "more often than not" a year after their loved one died. The bereaved must also show six of the following: (1) difficulty accepting the death, (2) disbelief or emotional numbness, (3) difficulty with positive reminiscing about the deceased, (4) bitterness or anger about the loss, (5) self-blame and its variants, (6) avoidance of others, (7) social disruption, (8) a desire to die, (9) difficulty trusting others, (10) feeling alone or that life is meaningless, (11) a diminished sense of identity, and (12) a reluctance to pursue interests. With a list of criteria this long, it's easy to imagine someone meeting six of them, even after a year.

The American Psychiatric Association reports that in a given year nearly one in five US adults experience some form of mental illness.[28] Of all the diagnoses, grief seems to be the most resistant to being called a disease, in part because lots of lay-people believe it's normal to love strongly and grieve deeply. Many of us, including some mental health professionals, just do not feel comfortable consigning grief—which we think of as a universal experience—to a book of medical disorders. Still, despite our broad sympathy for this particular type of *dolor*, since 2010 researchers have performed clinical trials on what pharmaceutical companies will eventually brand as grief medication.[29]

Assuming I outlive some of my cherished loved ones, there's a good chance I'll fall into the category of people diagnosable with complicated grief, just as surely as Marcia and Montaigne would if they were being assessed today. I will probably also be prescribed an extra dose of shame, not just from society but from the medical community. The *Diagnostic and Statistical Manual of Mental Disorders* is like a new, scientific Seneca, telling "complicated" grievers that over 95 percent of other grievers get over it sooner. The pressure to heal before twelve months have elapsed is likely to be one of the causes of my extended grief.

Seneca may have shamed Marcia, but he did not medicalize her grief. He just thought it wasn't reasonable. Cicero agreed with Seneca that grief is irrational, that it is just "a matter of (bad) opinion like any number of 'perturbations of the mind.'"[30] But then he took one more step. In the *Tusculan Disputations*, Cicero devoted a whole chapter to calling grief a product of a "swollen" or "inflamed" mind.[31] Wise men, Cicero wrote, can sometimes fall into temporary hysterics, "raving" or feeling "furor," but they would still count as sane because they remain governed by their reason. In contrast, he said, we would have to be sick to grieve. Insanity, believed Cicero, is escaping from under the thumb of reason.

Unlike Aristotle, who argued for a moderate amount of emotion, Cicero wanted none of it.[32] Negative emotions in particular were evidence to him of a sick mind—the ancient Roman equivalent of a brain disease.[33] And it is not only negative emotions that can drive us crazy, he thought, but positive ones too, like desire and joy. Cicero would probably have diagnosed Montaigne with a "swollen" mind even while La Boétie lived: they loved each other too ravenously to be healthy. Emotions make us demented, thought Cicero. They literally take us out of our minds, leaving our bodies running around doing God knows what.

Even small emotions are dangerous, though Cicero knew from experience that grief is anything but small and in fact is a particularly nasty type of distress.[34] One reason he knew this— and a major reason why Cicero's friends considered him a bad Stoic—is that, when it was his turn, he failed miserably at grief. In 45 BCE, Cicero's daughter Tullia died. He came very close to building her a shrine, and he up and left his wife after suspecting that she liked the new Tullia-free arrangement.[35] He wallowed in self-pity.[36] Cicero's friend Brutus wrote a letter telling him just how un-Stoically he was grieving and asking him to please get his shit together. As one commentator put it, Cicero responded to the Brutuses in his life by becoming "belligerent and resentful of friends and colleagues who urged him to remit his grieving, or alleged that grief had impaired his mental state."[37] Cicero was determined to grieve hard.

But he was also determined to grieve Stoically. Cicero wrote his philosophy of grief in the midst of his grief, and he thought he was doing a pretty good job of "manning up." Here he was, two months out from Tullia's death (presumably still operating under an inflamed mind), when he wrote a treatise on grief. He swore that he was doing two good things: (1) distracting himself with writing, and (2) pretending not to be sad. So desperate was Cicero to be a Stoic that he could not even admit to indulging the "weak and womanish" part of himself that sorely missed his daughter.[38]

And yet Cicero must have suspected that his friends were right. He had theoretically agreed that we save ourselves heartache and headache when we correct our perception of death and get on with life. But here he was, fiercely and embarrassingly believing that his daughter's death was bad. He had been the one to suggest felling the tree of grief and destroying it at the roots, but he couldn't even hold the ax.[39] For mental wellness, Cicero thought, a person needs to get a hold of themselves. He just couldn't do it.

One way to get hold of yourself, Cicero thought, is by reading and discussing philosophy. As we saw, Seneca said the same thing in his consolation letters a century later. Although there are drawbacks to thinking of philosophy as medicine for the soul, Cicero and Seneca were both right that philosophy can help us—though not if we are going to start by calling grief a dark and effeminate tree that needs chopping down.[40]

To seal his fate as a man who suffered from grief as a mental illness, Cicero was posthumously diagnosed by the modern-day scholar Kathleen Evans with perhaps, statistically speaking, the most feminized of mental illnesses: major depressive disorder.[41] The Stoic idea that grief is irrational still has considerable purchase in psychiatry, but it has evolved over time. In 1651, Robert Burton called grief a "transitory melancholy," that is, a physical disease.[42] In 1917, Sigmund Freud shot back, arguing that grief is no illness. "Although mourning involves great departures from the normal attitude to life," he conceded, "it never occurs to us to regard it as a pathological condition and to refer it to medical treatment."[43] Freud even believed that messing with someone's grief process could hurt them.[44] Emil Kraepelin—the father of psychiatry and Freud's rival—disagreed. He decided that grief is an illness, and he won.[45] Kraepelin is a major reason why grief is physicalized, pathologized, and, with grief medication trials now underway, soon to be monetized.[46]

The "bereavement exclusion" in the fourth edition of the *Diagnostic and Statistical Manual of Mental Disorders* distinguished between depression-like symptoms resulting from the loss of a loved one and depression itself. This distinction served to keep grief (which has a known cause) separate from depression (which often does not). Until 2013, when the *DSM-5* was published, psychologists in the United States treated grief like Freud did—as part of the human condition.

But psychologists started to wonder: Since grief shares symptoms with major depressive disorder, wasn't it more responsible to treat them the same? After all, if someone looks depressed, does it really matter if they have a "valid excuse"?

Don't they suffer just the same? This logic was persuasive enough that a group of psychiatrists were called upon to settle the issue. They were tasked with deciding whether to keep the bereavement exclusion or remove it.

Against removing the bereavement exclusion were people who believed that grieving sometimes looks like depression. But it's important to put grief in context: someone you love has died, and you are naturally and/or reasonably having a hard time with this loss. People in this camp worried about what they called the "medicalization of normality" and rejected the move to pathologize grief.[47]

Overdiagnosis is not the problem, said the other side, nor should we worry that grievers will automatically start getting treated as depressives. The real problem, they said, is access to medication and therapy. Insurance companies require documentation, and a grieving person who needs a medical diagnosis in order to get help should be eligible for one (even if it leads to overdiagnosis).[48] "Loss is loss," this group says; there is no hierarchy of suffering.[49] For too many years, they maintain, the bereavement exclusion has, unwittingly, privileged grievers, situating them above depressives who can offer no reason for their depression. Grievers have been treated as the golden-haired kids, they say, standing next to those portrayed as their scraggly (probably lazy) siblings who have no legitimate excuse for their symptoms. Unlike grievers, depressives can't say, "I'm not mentally ill, I'm just grieving!" If we remove the exclusion, the logic goes, we combat our internalized perception that depression is weakness.

In 2013, the bereavement exclusion was removed from the *DSM*. Now grievers are eligible to receive a diagnosis of major depressive disorder if they show signs of depression for more than two weeks.[50]

Which side of the issue you take depends on whether you believe that mental illness refers to a group of symptoms or to a contextual set of feelings and behaviors. It also depends on how much you trust the medical establishment. Assuming your doctor has good motives and plenty of time to counsel you over multiple visits that last longer than the standard ten minutes, you might not be worried about receiving a hasty depression diagnosis. If you're diagnosed with depression after two weeks of grieving, you are one of the 0.5 percent of the population who would have been denied treatment prior to 2013.[51] But if you don't want to call your grief depression (even if you meet six of the criteria), you might feel that your grief has been pathologized. In a world where healthy means happy, contented, joyful, functional, back-to-work—light—your closed blinds on week three will look pretty unhealthy to our medical establishment.

It is undeniable that grievers suffer. It's also undeniable that they are shamed by a culture that feels more comfortable seeing our blinds open. It's easy to see why someone would feel broken if they have been convinced that "normal" people grieve for two weeks and then start to lighten up. It's easy to imagine a person shattered by grief calling themselves disordered, sick, and broken. The plight of grievers compels us to ask: Can we interrupt the Light Metaphor so that it does not give rise to the Brokenness Story? Is there another story of grief that we can tell to shift our society's perception of it?

———

When C. S. Lewis married Joy Gresham, he knew that he would watch her die. He did not know that it would take four years, nor that grief would shatter his faith.

Lewis and Gresham married in the hospital where Joy was being treated for cancer. It was 1956, by which time everyone had assumed that the fifty-eight-year-old Lewis would never marry. The priest who married them laid hands on Joy, and her cancer went into remission. This gave the Lewises almost four years to live as man and wife, but it also made his grief over her death look outsized to everyone who thought Joy was just a friend. Lewis did what many grievers do: he fell apart. He also did what few of them do: he wrote a book about it.

A Grief Observed bears witness to the depth of sadness, anger, and confusion that grief stirred in Lewis. The book is a mirror, stared into by souls sitting in the darkness of grief, but it's also a window for featherweights like me who do not yet know what it feels like to have the soul of a deceased loved one sewn into one's flesh. There is no light to be found in *A Grief Observed*, only a man wrestling with God and himself in the dark. The book's greatest lesson is that grieving is part of living. The context, however, is everything.

Lewis was an author made famous by his cocksure faith in God. When Joy died, he reports watching his faith—now a house of cards—collapse.[52] Instead of reverting to his childhood atheism, though, Lewis became a "wild cat" who "growled and spit at the operator."[53] By turns, Lewis called God a vivisectionist, a Cosmic Sadist, and a spiteful imbecile.[54] His vitriol toward God must have surprised him, but his faith had never been tested like this before.

"I thought I trusted the rope until it mattered to me whether it would bear me," Lewis observed. "Now it matters, and I find I didn't."[55]

Eventually, Lewis found that the door between him and God was "no longer shut and bolted." But he wondered if his house of cards would fall again when his own body gave way. It didn't, but he would not find that out for two years.[56]

Lewis's grief, in addition to pummeling his faith, unmasked an overly simplistic theology. For years, he had told people that their deceased loved ones were in a "better place." He had assumed, as many people still do, that these words brought comfort to grievers. But he came to find out that the baton of condolence he'd been passing along for years was splintered. Lewis experienced firsthand how inept his consolations had always been, and how dangerous.

Lewis's default consolation had been religious in nature, which was why he violently rejected it when one of his friends or colleagues would try to pass that baton to him. Whenever someone said that Joy was in a better place or that he would reunite with her after his death—whenever they tried to bring him into the light—he would hiss back in response:

> Talk to me about the truth of religion and I'll listen gladly. Talk to me about the duty of religion and I'll listen submissively. But don't come talking to me about the consolations of religion or I shall suspect you don't understand.[57]

The idea that everything earthly would be regained in the afterlife—that there would be "cigars in heaven"—revolted Lewis because that was precisely what he wanted.[58] It was also exactly what he could no longer bring himself to believe. No amount of sugar could get him to swallow the pill of faith that he had so joyfully administered to readers and followers before Joy's death.

If you think, like Seneca, Cicero, and the younger Lewis, that grief is an invasive tree that threatens the forest, chances are you will move quickly to chop it down. But if you think that your grief is what keeps your love from evaporating, as Marcia,

Montaigne, and the older Lewis might have, you will have a hard time grieving in a world that keeps handing you axes. No number of friends trying to drag Lewis into the sweet light of Christianity helped. Bringing a torch to light his cave did not work, but it did shame him. *A Grief Observed* is a great book, not because it perfectly captures grief, but because it perfectly captures the shame of grief brought on by loved ones who wish to offer nothing more than light.

Two thousand years after Cicero lost his daughter Tullia, Lewis came face to face with the same gulf Cicero encountered—the gulf between what he thought he believed and what he really believed, between what he wanted to believe and what he could believe. This is the gulf that finds all of us in surprising ways. Like Cicero, Lewis thought he knew who he was, but then his person died.

Even as he wrote the book, Lewis was aware of being an embarrassment to everyone he encountered.[59] He sensed he was making his friends and acquaintances uncomfortable, but he did not hide his sadness. Lewis could tell that people did not want to see his deep and dark feelings. He didn't want to see them himself. So when Lewis was not busy calling God a spiteful imbecile, he was flagellating himself for indulging his self-pity. "Feelings, and feelings, and feelings. Let me try thinking instead."[60] As an intellectual and a human, Lewis was torn between thinking and feeling, caught falling apart but wishing he could keep it together.

As a young man who had seen the evils of war and the mental devastation it caused the surviving soldiers, Lewis had resolved to pay little attention to his inner life. In a letter he wrote shortly after the war, he advised his friend and comrade to "keep clear of introspection and brooding. Keep to work and sanity and open air. . . . We hold our mental health by a thread, and nothing is worth risking for it."[61] As a young man, Lewis tried not to jeopardize his mental health by indulging his feelings; as an older man, he let loose. Just as the young Lewis believed that masturbating was a mortal sin but still did it frequently and with much fervor, the older Lewis could not keep away from his grief, despite having resolved not to stroke it.

In the introduction to *A Grief Observed*, Lewis's stepson Douglas Gresham corrected a long-standing misunderstanding between him and Jack (as friends called Lewis). Lewis had written that whenever he tried to talk about Joy with his two stepsons, "there appears on their faces neither grief, nor love, nor pity, but the most fatal of all non-conductors, embarrassment. They look as if I were committing an indecency."[62] So as to spare them embarrassment, Lewis resolved not to talk to them about grief or Joy anymore. But Gresham reports that what Lewis had interpreted as the face of embarrassment was in fact shame.

"I knew that if Jack talked to me about Mother, I would weep uncontrollably and, worse still, so would he." Gresham blamed his seven-year "indoctrination" by the British preparatory school system, which taught him that "the most shameful thing that could happen to me would be to be reduced to tears in public."[63] Today we would call the lesson Gresham absorbed as a boy "toxic masculinity"; we know it's not just British boys who are taught not to cry. But the mid-twentieth-century ideal of a "strong man" certainly left boys and men alike to grieve and feel shame alone. It was particularly tragic in the case of the Gresham boys, who were teenagers when their mother died.[64] Their grief had no acceptable outlet, and Douglas Gresham reported that it took him thirty years to cry without feeling shame.[65] Stifled boys become stifled men who have been told to stop crying like a girl, as my son's baseball coach told his son—in 2021.

Lewis was right to be ashamed of his rawness from grief, in the sense that he read the room right. But he also thought his embarrassingly honest book might help people. He had trouble finding a publisher. T. S. Eliot didn't want to touch the book until he found out it was written by Lewis, and even then, he published it pseudonymously. As predicted, *A Grief Observed* by "N. W. Clerk" bombed. The archbishop of York reportedly called it "mawkish and unmanly" because it exposed so many dark feelings.[66] As the Lewis biographer A. N. Wilson put it, "no one seemed sure that N. W. Clark [*sic*], whoever he was, should be allowed to burden the world with his unhappiness."[67] The reading public was not ready, in 1961, for the level of *dolor* expressed in *A Grief Observed*. They didn't have enough emotional literacy to appreciate what critics complained was a "very private document."[68]

Grief-shaming twice-curses grievers: people who are already suffering the pains of grief are made to feel worse about their pain, as though the very act of grieving makes them weaklings. Seneca shamed Marcia. Brutus shamed Cicero. The Brits shamed Lewis. Grief-shame is based on the bright idea that grief is a broken mood.

———

On the top shelf of the hall closet in the house I grew up in lived a mysterious-looking shoebox. I was five or so when I saw it for the first time, but even then, I knew that I was not to open it. My sister told me it was full of consolation cards addressed to my parents after the death of my brother, six years before I was born. No one ever talked to me about him, and everything I knew I learned by studying the photo on the hutch built into the fireplace. Before I turned nine, I was younger than him.

One day I was older. He looks like a sweet child. This is what I know.

Either it was too painful for my parents to talk about my brother or they believed they should not talk about him for our sake, their unborn children included. In any case, because they never talked about him, I did not grow up competing with a ghost. I never had to shoulder the weight of my parents' sadness or wonder if they would trade me to have him back. My childhood came out looking no different from the childhoods of my friends whose parents didn't get crushed together in that particular mortar. My parents made a choice to live for their remaining eight children instead of die with the one who was gone. If they had been overcome by grief, they could have been lost to us. I might not have been born.

My parents' decision to keep my brother in a box on the shelf in the closet was respectable and responsible. It was loving. They were lucky not to have suffered over the long term, as Marcia and Montaigne did. They got back to work and life. They put the past behind them. They laughed again and went on to live long and happy lives, free from mental illness. My parents make good Stoics inadvertently, and good Catholics intentionally. They chose to walk in the light.

Still, I heard rumors that, once upon a time, my father used to get on the floor to play with his children. I heard that in another life my mother used to play the guitar for them. I once asked her about it, and she told me that she stopped playing "when the boy died." Grief leaves its mark on a family even as we try to soldier through it. What is the cost of silence? What gets lost in the light?

Imagine if C. S. Lewis's embarrassing honesty were the new normal, except without the shame. Imagine him talking to his stepsons about Joy daily. Better yet, imagine that the British

preparatory schools and American T-ball teams did not indoc-
trinate children with the idea that boys don't cry. Imagine a
United States more influenced by Lewis than by Seneca, a culture that keeps its dead close and talks about them even after
the funeral. What would it look like if we were allowed to incor-
porate loss into our daily lives, if we pushed light aside to make
a little room for darkness?

In 2017, the grief therapist Megan Devine wrote *It's OK That
You're Not OK: Meeting Grief and Loss in a Culture That Doesn't
Understand*, which lays out story after story of botched condolences that either blame the bereaved or shame them. Here's a
selection.

- At least you had them for as long as you did.
- You can always have another child/find another partner.
- They're in a better place now.
- At least now you get to know what's really important
  in life.
- This will make you a better person in the end.
- You won't always feel this bad.
- You're stronger than you think.
- This is all part of the plan.
- Everything happens for a reason.[69]

In her experience, Devine says, few people respond to grievers in a way that does not pile onto their grief, so she created an
animated video instructing viewers on what to say instead of
these unhelpful platitudes.[70] The problem with these attempts
at condolence, Devine points out, is that they suggest an unspo-
ken ending. "You are stronger than you think" tacitly ends with
"so stop feeling how you feel."[71] Onlookers don't want to see us
hurt—for a million reasons, including self-concern—so they

try to rush us through it. Devine herself was accused of being too sad and too angry for too long when her life partner died unexpectedly. Writing from personal and professional experience, she describes a world where darkness is not tolerated except by some grievers. Devine's book, her website, and her thirty-day writing course are meant to provide a haven for grievers who have been shamed by a culture that makes grief harder. "Grief is not a problem to be fixed," she writes. "It's an experience to be carried."[72]

Lewis's friends tried to fix his problem by dragging him out of the dark, but he resisted. Instead of accepting their penny aphorisms so he could get over his wife's death and get back to work, he sat in the dark and wrote what he saw there.

A Grief Observed is Lewis's antidote to grief-shaming, even though he felt ashamed of his grief. It's a stubborn invitation to readers to stop thinking of grief as a tree that needs to be felled, as well as a lesson in emotional literacy from a man who was far from fluent. *A Grief Observed* wisely rejects the Light Metaphor even though its author was partly under its sway. To read it is to watch an intellectual giant fail to conquer his grief and give the rest of us permission to stop trying.[73] Lewis left us a big shady tree under which to sit with our grief, should we choose to.

Despite his own protests, Lewis showed us what it is to be raw, to doubt, to love recklessly, and to fall apart. His grief is an alternative to the Stoic griever who distracts himself by keeping busy. It's an alternative to the Brokenness Story, which says that grievers need fixing. Lewis refused to hide from his emotions (despite his shame over them) and then refused to keep them in his drawer (again, despite his shame). In publishing his sadness, doubt, hopelessness, anger, blasphemy, and shame, Lewis gave us permission to grieve hard.

We can learn from Lewis to do what he was unable to do in his historical moment: to grieve with dignity. A person in grief need not hang their head low because they are not bouncing back. That person is every bit as dignified as the widower who frenetically washes dishes. Death gets us all in the end. It is not possible to outrun *dolor*. There's always a trace left of it, like the silence when my mother set down the guitar. Grief is similar to the other difficult moods in that it comes for us, but unlike the others, grief is considered completely normal by a lot of people—at least theoretically, and for the first two weeks. Grief is not an indication that we have prepared badly or that we are responding to a death in the wrong way. Grief puts us in touch with a basic fact: surviving hurts. There are many ways to grieve, and we need not think of grief as a problem to be fixed or as a pathology. Like all the painful moods, grief is there to be sat with—Devine says "carried"—until we can see in the dark.

After Lewis's death in 1963, *A Grief Observed* was rereleased under his real name. Sales shot up.[74] Maybe Lewis's readers loved him enough to let him be sad, maybe they were a bit sadistic, or maybe they were eager to learn from him. For a long time, the deceased Lewis was one of only a few public voices who tacitly advocated for trying to see in the dark instead of turning on a light. Today there are more such voices, including some well-known public figures.

In an interview, a visibly shaken Anderson Cooper, who was grieving the very recent loss of his mother, asked Stephen Colbert, whose father and two brothers died in a plane crash over forty years ago, to talk about how he deals with that loss today. When Colbert told Cooper that the greatest outcome of his suffering was that it enabled him to relate to other grieving people, he probably didn't know that he was channeling Unamuno—who had said we can see other people in *dolor* better when we are feeling *dolor* ourselves. Colbert is a person who can see in the dark. He knows there's no avoiding pain. Lewis was another.

Other contemporary examples of people who learned to stop dragging grievers into the light share the belief that grief is not a problem. Devine is one. Nora McInerny is another. She lost her husband to brain cancer and had to deal with the kind of botched condolences that Devine lists. McInerny has written books about living with—not despite—loss. She also hosts the podcast *Terrible, Thanks for Asking,* a public platform intent on not giving stories an artificially happy ending.

Elisabeth Kübler-Ross, well known for her often misunderstood stages of grief (she never meant them to be taken as sequential), recounted a story about a recently bereaved widow. This young woman was talking on the phone with her parents, and when she began to cry, her mother tried to get off the phone. She might have been trying to let her daughter grieve in private. "Luckily," writes Kubler-Ross, "her father jumped in and said, 'No. I'm staying on the line even though she's crying.'"[75] The father was willing to sit in the dark with his grieving daughter. Would that we all had someone who loved us enough not to hang up on us when we are feeling alone.

I once met a woman who told me, without any hint of sadness in her voice, that she likes to cry in the ocean. Her tears, she said, get conveniently washed away and no one has to know. She was defending a woman's right to grieve privately, making the argument that everyone grieves differently, and demonstrating that some people don't want to share their business with everyone. This argument makes sense. We do grieve differently. Today we might call a woman who cries only in the ocean strong and brave, or British. But in a hundred years, more hearts than mine will be pierced by a story like this. More of us will locate tragedy in the fact that, once upon a time, there lived a woman who sought comfort from the sea after having learned from experience that no human soul on land was competent to hold her sadness.

Maybe one day our society will realize that we cannot make difficult moods go away by stifling them, and that a desire for "privacy" is often born of neglected needs. Fred Rogers wrote:

> People have said "Don't cry" to other people for years and years, and all it has ever meant is "I'm too uncomfortable when you show your feelings: Don't cry." I'd rather have them say, "Go ahead and cry. I'm here to be with you."[76]

Perhaps one day we will not fear that sadness will drive our loved ones away and we will accept their emotional embraces. We will worry less about their discomfort than our own agony. We will reject the idea that talking about grief makes it last longer, and we'll stop saying that if we start crying, we'll "never stop." We will agree with the fourth-century Christian desert fathers (whom we'll hear from in the next chapter) that crying brings comfort, and we'll be equipped to hold one another's tears.[77] Maybe we'll even cry openly and without apology for "getting emotional" because we will have learned that crying is no more inappropriate, embarrassing, or contagious than laughing. Grieving out loud will not be seen as evidence of a failure to "keep it together." It will be treated as one dignified way that humans express their humanity while coming to grips with living.

chapter 4

recoloring depression

"How many of you are left-handed?" I ask my students for a show of hands. Out of a class of forty, three or four *zurdos* ("lefties") raise their hands, which seems about right, given that 10 percent of the population is left-handed. I speak directly to them.

"What's it like living in a world made for right-handed people?" The "righties" in the class furrow their brows. I empathize with their confusion as I watch them look around the classroom and notice all the right-handed desks, perhaps for the first time. Right-handed people tend not to notice the architecture of the world because it accommodates them. The physical world curves around their bodies' needs. As a righty from a family of righties, I do not judge the right-handed students for their ignorance. Like them, I was not aware that lefties had a completely different way of interacting with the world until I listened to their stories.

Two *zurdos* call out answers to my question. Both are seated in right-handed desks because that's all this room has.

"I've just learned to live with it," says Zaida, a long-haired sophomore with clear-rimmed glasses. She had twisted herself into an awkward sideways pose, the only way she can write with her left hand on a surface attached to the right side of her chair. She sees a few other students noticing and shrugs.

Jorge nods from the middle of the room. He's clean-cut and wears a button-down shirt and dress pants. Although he sits facing forward like his right-handed peers, he has had to balance a notebook on his lap to write. The right part of the desk is useless to him. He seems glad to have his discomfort noticed.

"It's always been this way, so I've gotten used to it." Such accommodation is not surprising, given that the left-handed minority bumps up against the physical world constantly. Every day lefties adjust their posture, their arms, and their fingers to fit scissors, keyboards, can openers, and computer mice.

These are small things, these students tell me, but they are reminders that there is only one world, and in it, the lefties have to adapt to the righties.

"Isn't it uncomfortable," I ask, "to always be backwards?"

"Yes," another *zurdo* admits. By this point, most of the righties are looking down at their desks. They see how the desks were designed with them in mind. Just like the US Capitol Building with its 365 steps was built with walking people in mind.[1] Just like spacesuits and crash test dummies were created with men in mind.

"Emotional lefties," including people who live with chronic, clinical, or even mild depression, live in a world shaped by the Light Metaphor. In the light of religion, depression looks like a sin—despair—in which you turn away from God. In the light of consumerism, or capitalism, or positive thinking, depression looks like weakness, laziness, or a plain failure to get to work. Depression is a *dolor* far more perplexing than grief because, in most cases, nobody has died. As Andrew Solomon, author of

The Noonday Demon: An Atlas of Depression, described his first episode of depression, he could find "no excuse for it under the circumstances."[2] It came on as boredom after he finished writing what would become a very successful book. Over the next few weeks, the boredom degenerated into a debilitating depression.

People with depression have suffered a brutal history of not being taken seriously, so the light of science is a welcome alternative to the previous lights. In the light of science, depression doesn't look like a choice, or sin, or laziness, or the blues. It doesn't look like something a person can will themselves to "get over." Instead, it looks real, cruel, debilitating. The American Psychological Association reports that depression (both major and minor) is the most common of the mental disorders, and that women suffer more from it than men. It's a maladaptive mood, a broken system, says Solomon. These words can be very comforting to a person whose prior vocabulary offered them only a choice between "sinner" and "loser." Clinical depression can be harrowing. It can leave a sufferer like Solomon unable to answer the phone, shower, or even cut up his own food. The opposite of depression, he found out, is not happiness but vitality, the energy that allows a person to feel sadness, joy, or any emotion at all "without nullity."[3]

In 2022, depression can be treated. The American Psychological Association reports that the right combination of therapy and medication "can help ensure recovery."[4] And although Solomon calls the medications available today "primitive," not very effective, expensive, and likely to cause terrible side effects, these meager offerings have nonetheless saved countless lives. Solomon says he's grateful to be living now, when we have access to medications, instead of in earlier times when people just had to suffer through their depression.[5] When the book *Plato, Not Prozac!* was published in 1999, it suggested that we don't need medication, that all we need is philosophy to help us get through dark times.[6] Today it makes more sense to change that title to *Plato and Prozac*. If medication helps us feel sadness without nullity, then it makes sense to use it.

But this chapter is not about medication; it's about language. Just as it's hard to name and talk about the harmful side effects of our brightest beliefs about anger, sadness, and grief, it's tricky to ask whether the current vocabulary we use for depression helps or hurts. Does it do any harm to label depression—which can range from the melodramatic but arguably less life-threatening wail "I'm so depressed!" to Andrew Solomon's experience of not being able to cut up his own food—a kind of brokenness? Is it possible that the dominant story we tell about depression has something to do with why, in 2021, one in three college freshmen were diagnosed with it?[7] Finally, what do we do with the undeniable fact that the brokenness language was in part created and is now sustained by a multibillion-dollar pharmaceutical industry that profits from selling us a fix?[8] Who benefits when depression is marketed as a disease?

Questions like mine can be read as threatening or insulting, for good reason: some people do not "believe" in mental illness. They see moods like depression as weakness or even as the modern invention of a spoiled class. *Everyone gets sad. Shouldn't we just tough it out?* These people, who are highly influenced by a culture with little tolerance for darkness, would be classified as anti-medical, and I do not share their view. The light of medicine has helped millions of people gain access to medication and therapy, miraculous interventions that save lives. I do not suggest turning off this light.

But can we dim it? Can we ask: What is the cost we pay for thinking of depression *exclusively* as a mental illness? When depression is disease, it looks like something we should obliterate, as Peter Kramer advocates in *Against Depression*. He insists that we need to stop romanticizing depression and finally set out to vanquish it.[9] But given that obliterating the disease is not always possible without obliterating its host, do we have no other choice but to eternally consign depressed people to the company of the "Broken and Beautiful" that Kelly Clarkson sang about in 2019? When depression looks like a brain disease, those who suffer from it look sick, broken, and in need of fixing. A student once wrote to me that he was not a normal teenager because he needed medication for depression. I replied with the suggestion that he might be a normal teenager who needs medication. Too many people still equate diagnosis with dysfunction, but in the case of depression they need the diagnosis to get the help they need.

Are there other ways to see and talk about depression? Can we imagine recognizing a person's suffering, and giving them access to help, without asking them to see themselves as broken? What would it take for the emotional *zurdos* in my class to see themselves as dignified, and not in spite of their depression? Maybe dignity is hardest to see in the light of the sun. Maybe it's easier to see in the moonlight.

————

Gloria Anzaldúa was a *zurda* who suffered from what today would likely be diagnosed as clinical depression. She lived in a world where depressed people were expected to "think positive" just as surely as gay people were expected to "act straight." Like my left-handed students, Anzaldúa was raised in a world that did not fit her. As a child growing up in the 1950s in the South Texas borderlands, she was a dark horse emotionally, physically, and otherwise. Her voracious reading habit upset her mother, who knew only how to love a good little Mexican girl who dusted lamps and mopped floor tiles; she was perplexed by this untraditional little tomboy who preferred to paint and read instead. Even as a young girl, Anzaldúa knew she would never iron clothes for a husband or braid the hair of a squirming daughter. She was going to spend her life reading, writing, and painting. She would give birth to ideas.

In her elementary school backpack, Anzaldúa kept books written by Søren Kierkegaard and Friedrich Nietzsche. Even at so young an age, she knew that *prietas* like her did not read authors like these.[10] Her prized books were not written with a Spanglish-speaking Mexican field worker like her in mind, any more than student desks were designed with lefties in mind. Still, her intellectual appetite was insatiable. "I was that kind of kid," she remembers.[11]

At twenty-one, Anzaldúa enrolled in Texas Women's University, leaving her family for the first time to devote herself to the hundreds of dead poets, writers, and painters who had become her life. None of the artists looked, spoke, or wrote like her, so she started thinking of herself as different, a little off. She got on a bus headed north, hoping to find *el mundo zurdo*, the world made for left-handed folks like her. She had to come home after a year when she could no longer afford tuition, but by continuing to work in the fields and saving money, she was able to attend and graduate from Pan American College. It's the legacy institution of the University of Texas Rio Grande Valley (UTRGV), where I now teach. If I had been teaching in 1967, Anzaldúa would have been my student. (Of course, there were no Latinas teaching philosophy at my university in 1967.)

The worlds that Anzaldúa encountered "out there" did not fit her any better than the one she left. None of the cities she lived in would ever smell as good or be as warm to the touch as a homemade tortilla, the kind she dreamed of while living in Vermont and planning her first book.[12] Living the life of a queer and homesick writer, she was the gay person among straights in North and South Texas, the *Tejana* in San Francisco, the dark-skinned farmworker among white academics in Vermont, and the short Mexican with the strange accent in Indiana and Brooklyn. She eventually made a home for herself in Santa Cruz, California, "the dyke capital of the world," but even there she compared herself to a turtle who always carries home on its back.[13] She hauled not just her precious books from city to city but also her cultures, her languages, and her imagination.

When Anzaldúa died at sixty-one, she was a famous author and speaker who was treated by her fellow graduate students as though she were their teacher. In addition to publishing *Borderlands/La Frontera: The New Mestiza*, she had coedited three groundbreaking scholarly collections, written three children's books, and given enough interviews to form a published volume. As evidenced by the American Studies Association's Lifetime Achievement Award (2001) and a Google Doodle on what would have been her seventy-fifth birthday (September 26, 2017), Anzaldúa's legacy continues to inspire.

But despite all of Anzaldúa's accolades, home wasn't the only thing she carried on her back. Like many of us, she carried *dolores*. She was born with a rare condition that started her menses at three months old. Every twenty-four days, little Gloria would menstruate for ten intensely painful days. She had to keep it a secret, even from her siblings, because it was considered freakish and dirty.[14] With this condition came an early puberty: her breasts started growing at the age of six, and pubic hair stuck out of her shorts during PE at school.[15] "Keep your legs shut, *Prieta*," she remembers her mother saying.[16]

Anzaldúa's father died when she was fourteen.[17] She had four near-death experiences herself, including almost drowning at South Padre Island. As an adult, Anzaldúa was mugged twice and had a hysterectomy at age thirty-eight. On top of all that, she developed diabetes, which caused neuropathy, dizziness, headaches, and difficulty seeing.[18] Reflecting on it all later, Anzaldúa admitted that, from the physical to the mental, "pain was a way of life, my normal way of life."[19]

Anzaldúa also carried around a feeling of being an "alien from another planet."[20] As a child, she was expected to fill what she thought of as the "traditional" role for a Mexican woman, but it was clear from the beginning that she would not. Instead of obeying her mother's orders to iron her brothers' shirts, fix them dinner, and serve them food, she went off reading, painting, digging ditches, and hunting snakes.[21] Even cooking, which she enjoyed as a child, took time away from her reading, so she stopped doing it.[22] Little Gloria knew what she liked, and she did it without apology, even when people gave her hell for it.

But neither was she immune to feeling "embarrassed" when her mother would tell friends that all she did was lie in bed reading instead of helping with the housework.[23] Gloria admitted to being the most disobedient of the four children in the family, the rebel, the black sheep. But she always also sensed that she was just being herself.[24] She was ambivalent. Her sister and mother might have called her "selfish" for wanting to develop her mind instead of ironing her brothers' clothes, but to Gloria "selfish" was what people called you when you didn't do what they wanted you to do. It took her thirty years to learn this, during which time she felt a tremendous amount of guilt.[25]

The guilt Anzaldúa felt extended to her writing, even as an adult. When a depressive episode would hit, she became incapable of washing dishes, answering the phone, or responding to email. Her story was always the same. She would lock herself inside herself and swallow the key. It's no wonder that, as a small child, Anzaldúa found in Søren Kierkegaard (whom we'll hear from in the next chapter) "a despair equaling [her] own."[26] More than a hundred years earlier, Kierkegaard had described a lake that was endlessly deep beyond the overgrown marsh protecting it. At the bottom of the lake was a locked wooden box, with the key inside it. *Indesluttethed*, a kind of "despairing silence," was what Kierkegaard called this "self-encapsulation," or "inclosing of oneself."[27] Like so many of us, Anzaldúa could relate to the idea of getting locked inside herself.

During these dark times, Anzaldúa would revert back to what she had understood to be her limitations, which were inevitably framed by other people's expectations. "Who am I," Anzaldúa asked herself, "a poor, *Chicanita* from the sticks, to think I could write?" As she heard the words "selfish," "lazy," and "*consentida*" (spoiled) repeating in her head, she would feel more and more incapacitated. Anzaldúa's depressive episodes turned up the volume on the voices of her childhood. She was supposed to be someone's wife and mother, not a depressed Chicana who couldn't *levantar cabeza* (lift up her head).[28] As she told Inés Hernández-Ávila, a Native American studies professor and fellow *Tejana*, in an interview, "We were never supposed to write."[29]

A diagnosis of type 1 diabetes at age fifty further triggered Anzaldúa's depression. She recalls going through a year of denial and resistance to the idea of being sick yet again—"Did I deserve this? Where did I fuck up?" But she began to study her illness as diligently as she studied poetry, Chicana theory, feminism, philosophy, and astrology. She saved daily records of what she ate, what she should eat, her glucose levels, and how she felt. Her record-keeping helped her avoid becoming hypo-glycemic, which could make her lose consciousness if she failed to balance out her blood sugar in time. Even if only a little hy-poglycemic, Anzaldúa found it hard to see, and therefore to write.[30]

Coping with diabetes and depression, Anzaldúa always had less energy than she thought she would or should have. Dead-lines were tough to meet because it always took her longer to finish a piece than she had planned. Anzaldúa called it "rebel-ling" when she worked on something other than what had an impending deadline, but her friend and collaborator AnaLouise Keating called it giving in to "desire rather than deadlines."[31] As her coeditor on a book of essays, Keating correctly anticipated that Anzaldúa's essay would delay publication of the volume. Yet her work was always too good to leave behind.[32]

Like many people who suffer from energy-depleting conditions, Anzaldúa was misread. Colleagues who did not realize how sick and depressed she was gossiped that she had gotten too famous to attend academic conferences. De-pression and diabetes were twin burdens for Anzaldúa. They jeopardized her career as a "feminist-visionary-spiritual-activist-poet-philosopher fiction writer."[33] She recalled, "I went through periods of depression *y no podía hacer nada!* [I couldn't do anything!] I couldn't stay with a task because my eyes were bothering me. Dealing with my illness took all of my energy."[34] "At the beginning," she reported, "my friends were pissed because I wasn't interacting with them. I was so busy just surviving from day to day."[35] At first after she was diagnosed with diabetes, Anzaldúa could "hardly function" beyond taking care of herself, so she took herself out of the world for a year.[36]

In 2002, Anzaldúa emailed a poem about her depression to Keating. The poem, titled "Healing Wounds," reveals her state of mind as "the dirty dishes continue to pile up":

I have been ripped wide open
By a word, a look, a gesture—
From self, kin, and stranger.
My soul jumps out
Scurries into hiding
I hobble here and there
Seeking solace
Trying to coax it back home
But the me that's home
Has become an alien without it.
Wailing, I pull my hair
Suck snot back and swallow it
Place both hands over the wound
But after all these years
It still bleeds.[37]

Anzaldúa spent a lot of her time in darkness. As her poem recounts, she bled, she wailed, she pulled her hair. She tried to find solace, but often found anguish instead.

———

Despite how painful Anzaldúa's depression was, she did not call it a disorder, a disease, or an illness. Instead, she invented her own term for it. The Chicana artist took a subject as drab as clinical depression and made a colorful myth out of it. And just as Susan Cain created a theoretical space where introverts could stop feeling like failed extroverts by publishing *Quiet: The Power of Introverts in a World That Can't Stop Talking* in 2012, Anzaldúa published *Borderlands/La Frontera: The New Mestiza* in 1987 to create a theoretical space for Mexican Americans to stop feeling like failed Mexicans and failed Americans.[38] But *el mundo zurdo* was not only for them. It was for lefties of every kind. "In *El Mundo Zurdo* I with my own affinities and my people with theirs can live together and transform the planet."[39]

Today, *el mundo zurdo* would be home to LGBTQIA+ people who are kicked out of homophobic homes. It would welcome those among us who shade emotionally dark—those other people wish were sunnier. *El mundo zurdo* would not merely tolerate or accommodate people with depression, anxiety, anger, grief, and *dolor*. It would be built with them in mind, people whom she called "*almas afines*" (kindred spirits) who feel "excruciatingly alive to the world."[40]

In her early days of writing, Anzaldúa would sit naked under the California sun with a typewriter on her lap, growing darker and more vulnerable by the hour, "cultivating her colored skin."[41] But later she would write at night ("my night," she called it), by the light of the moon.[42] It was quiet then, a time that belonged not to the emotionally right-handed folks, who snored and drooled away the darkest hours, but to the *zurdos*. Those of us who are emotionally left-handed—depressed, anxious, angry, grieving, *dolorous*—often spend our nights awake and vigilant.

In the dark, Anzaldúa would meditate on darkness. In Aztec stories about the Earth's beginning, Anzaldúa found that darkness was revered as "the maternal, the germinal, the potential." In this beginning, darkness was not scary. But when the light split off, darkness became the villain, "identified with the negative, base and evil forces."[43] No longer would darkness be seen as maternal, a warm womb. From now on, darkness would be the enemy.

When Anzaldúa contemplated the origin of the universe, she sensed and articulated our contemporary society's bias against darkness in general, and dark skin specifically. She also came very close to invoking Plato's cave metaphor—so close that she might have had it in the back of her mind.[44] In describing how darkness could go from being "maternal" to "negative, base, and evil," Anzaldúa blames "the masculine order casting its dual shadow."[45] When Huitzilopochtli—the fiercely warlike sun god of Aztec mythology—made himself the hero of his own violent story, that was one shadow. But when he made darkness and the feminine traitorous enemies, he cast a second, or dual, shadow. If we think of Anzaldúa's origin story as a kind of Greco-Mexican hybrid metaphor, the sun is a dangerous puppeteer. He will not save us, but he will cast shadows on the wall that make us think night is bad and day is good, that women are negative and men are positive, that depression is black and health is white.

The bias against darkness that Anzaldúa describes is especially twisted when you consider *acedia*, depression's fourth-century cousin, which was said to strike not in darkness but in broad daylight. Acedia was originally one of "eight wicked thoughts" that afflicted the Christian desert fathers living in Egypt. It was the "noonday demon" of these monks, who described it as the feeling of wanting to run away from their cells. Part boredom, part apathy, and part malaise, acedia makes days feel interminable. When it strikes, you become convinced that your life is not for you, so you stop sweeping your cell and you start sleeping more. You stop praying to God and start devising an escape plan. Like depression, though, the noonday demon can possess you for months on end, during which time you are naked and alone, trapped inside yourself, burning in the sun instead of being gently warmed by it.

Acedia got axed from the list when the eight "wicked thoughts" became seven "vices" in the sixth century. For the next six hundred years, people forgot about acedia, or they considered it merely a monk's problem. Finally, in the twelfth century, Hugh of St. Victor brought acedia back from the dead and made it a capital sin. Saint Thomas Aquinas renamed it "sloth" and said it could take us straight to hell.[46]

Hardly anyone talks about acedia (or even sloth) anymore because contemporary science doesn't accept the idea that lethargy is a sin brought to you by the devil. Religion is no longer considered the arbiter of matters of the psyche. So it happened that acedia, formerly a sin inspired by a demon, turned into clinical depression, a disease induced by a brain malfunction or an unfortunate DNA strand.

A piece of wisdom we can take from the history of acedia— in addition to its being misread as "laziness," an attribute it shares with depression—is a suspicion of the sun. The hellish part of acedia is that, unlike fear, it does not go away when the sun comes up. Neither does depression. It makes sense that a depressed person would want to keep the blinds closed, since letting in the oppressive sun provides no relief. Why, then, would we ever call depression dark?

If we could get out from under the Light Metaphor, which has us convinced that light saves us, we might conclude that depression is more like an interminably long South Texas summer's day than a "dark night of the soul." Were the color white not historically claimed by light-skinned people who put dark-skinned people beneath them, it might be the clear choice for the color of depression—an overbearing whiteness that drives out all color.

Despite the racist bias against darkness, Anzaldúa remained faithful to the night. She made sense of her dark moods not by the light of the sun but by *la luna*. In the moon, Anzaldúa saw not a ball of gas or a piece of cheese, but the head of Coatlicue's daughter, Coyolxauhqui, the Earth goddess. Coyolxauhqui was sister to the sun, Huitzilopochtli, who threw her head into the night sky after she tried to kill their mother (or at least that was Huitzilopochtli's story). From that time until now, Huitzilopochtli rules the day as the sun, and Coyolxauhqui rules the night as the moon, helping people like Anzaldúa see in the dark.[47]

Coyolxauhqui's light is far softer than sunlight. She does not scare darkness away, nor does she find it dangerous. Anzaldúa calls the light of the moon her "medicine."[48] The title of the dissertation she died while still writing, *Light in the Dark/Luz en lo Oscuro*, refers to the moon, not the sun. The sun, the masculine, Huitzilopochtli, is blinding and violent for Anzaldúa, while the moon, the feminine, Coyolxauhqui, is maternal and good. Anzaldúa credits the moon for helping her see better in the dark.[49]

By the light of the moon, depression looked to Anzaldúa a lot like the Aztec goddess who swallows us whole and plunges us into darkness, but who gives us a new way to see. How often do we give credit to the moon, or even darkness itself, for insights?

In Aztec iconography, Coatlicue's head is made up of two rattlesnakes facing each other. They symbolize the giving and taking of life, because Coatlicue does both. She is both a womb and a "consuming internal whirlwind, the symbol of the underground aspects of the psyche."[50] Coatlicue is not kind. She is harsh, but Anzaldúa was used to harshness. Her sister tore up *Borderlands/La Frontera: The New Mestiza* and threw it into the garbage can, refusing to talk to her for three years.[51] Her mother made her feel lazy and freakish. But they also loved her. So it did not surprise Anzaldúa that her spiritual mother, Coatlicue, would catapult her into a depression multiple times over her lifetime.

Anzaldúa wrote that "when pain, suffering and the advent of death become intolerable," Coatlicue will "open and plunge us into its maw, devour us." Anzaldúa's goddess-mother grabbed hold of her and did not let go. When she found herself in Coatlicue's stomach, Anzaldúa realized that it was best to stay still. Deep thinking, or what she called "the ger-mination work," "takes place in the deep, dark earth of the unconscious." In the arms of Coatlicue, hidden ideas begin to surface. The unconscious mind begins to reveal itself.[52]

The "Coatlicue state" is not pretty. Anzaldúa wrote about the interaction between her diabetes and her depression, how hy-poglycemia would just "drag [her] down again." In an email, she wrote, "i let myself get too exhausted. spiritually and emotion-ally drained & now i'm paying for it. i sure wish i could learn to manage my life/work better."[53] Coatlicue was no simple friend to Anzaldúa, who went into her mother's arms only by getting dragged there.

Anzaldúa desperately needed to understand what was going on inside her depressive episodes, why she was there, and what she could learn. After all, she was a thinker. But she also loathed her compulsion to "try to make 'sense' of it all."[54] She finally came to believe there was only one way out of a depressive episode: to stop fighting it. Deep down, Anzaldúa believed that if she could let Coatlicue keep her from being productive for a few days, weeks, or months, she would be released. But still, she was always reluc-tant to "cross over, to make a hole in the fence and walk across, to cross the river, to take that flying leap into the dark."[55]

Anzaldúa was not keen on seeing in the dark if her teacher was Coatlicue. But neither would Coatlicue allow Anzaldúa to keep up the facade of productivity; she wouldn't even let Anzaldúa get out of bed every morning. Coatlicue made it impossible for Anzaldúa to ignore her spiritual pain. "Cradled in the arms of Coatlicue," Anzaldúa says, she was forced to dive into the "fecund cave of her imagination." As much as she did not want to admit, much less confront, her nasty feelings of selfishness and laziness, they overtook her body and made her incapable of normal everyday activities like washing dishes and socializing. Anzaldúa likened these experiences with Coatlicue to turning to stone and being unable to turn back into a human until she "kicked a hole out of the old boundaries." She would not be released from the bone-crushing arms of the stone goddess until she recognized that they were also a womb that could give birth to knowing some dark truth or seeing something new.

———

In *Borderlands/La Frontera: The New Mestiza*, Anzaldúa describes a central insight she gleaned in the dark of her depression. It centers on the perception that little Gloria had absorbed about herself—that she was selfish, *consentida*, lazy. Anzaldúa's painful time with Coatlicue showed her where her perception was off. She was not, in fact, lazy. She might not have given her life to plowing and picking as a migrant farmworker, but she had dug into herself to sow, water, and fertilize seeds of wisdom in her soul. From her labor grew essays and books that would change millions of people's lives, not least of all my students' lives. Deep down, Anzaldúa knew that to reject the colonial story that Mexicans who don't work the fields are lazy, she would need to immerse herself in precolonial myths.

Coatlicue showed Anzaldúa where her perception *had* been accurate. If industrious Americans saw what she did in her work as a writer (taking walks, meditating, reading books), as well as what she didn't do (writing for eight to ten hours straight, getting her hands dirty), they might think she was lazy. Her editors and publishers must have been displeased when she missed deadlines and might have easily concluded that she was misusing her time. But Anzaldúa dug deeper. The story of her laziness was not idiosyncratic to her. Anglos called Mexicans lazy long before the Mexican-American War ended in 1848, long before northwest Mexico became the American Southwest.

Cradled in the arms of Coatlicue, it occurred to Anzaldúa that, as a "second class member of a conquered people," people who looked like her had been "taught to believe they were inferior because they have indigenous blood, believe in the supernatural, and speak a deficient language." Anzaldúa realized that,

> as a person, I, as a people, we, Chicanos, blame ourselves, hate ourselves, terrorize ourselves. Most of this goes on unconsciously; we only know that we are hurting, we suspect that there is something "wrong" with us, something fundamentally "wrong."[56]

Anzaldúa believed this story for too long, and her belief plunged her even deeper into guilt and shame. But at her emotional rock bottom, she was able to connect her personal experience of feeling like a failure (today we might say "imposter") to the historical fact that her people had been made to feel like failures for centuries. Because of lingering biases against Indians dating back to the Spanish conquest, Chicanos and other nonwhites who strive to be artists, writers, or academics are given a script saying that their depression indicates that something is wrong with them rather than with the world. If they were not so self-indulgent and spoiled, they would be out picking oranges or strawberries or lettuce for real artists and writers. Coatlicue taught Anzaldúa that her shame did not come from a personal inability to keep deadlines. It came from the myth of the lazy Mexican, brought to her by a racist and sexist society obsessed with production.

All depressed artists are vulnerable to being called lazy, but Anzaldúa suffered the added burden of being a depressed Mexican artist, which got her classified as super-lazy. "All her life she's been told that Mexicans are lazy," so "she has had to work twice as hard as others to meet the standards of the dominant culture which have, in part, become her standards."[57] Anzaldúa had internalized the standard imposed on her people by colonizers and their descendants. Coatlicue freed her precisely by plunging her into darkness. There, far from the "light" of colonial standards, she could give birth to her own standards.

With this knowledge gained from the Coatlicue state, Anzaldúa hoped to stop "beating herself over the head" with the laziness trope. Coatlicue helped her realize that casting inactivity as a personal weakness had been a mistake. Inactivity, Anzaldúa realized as she matured, is "a stage as necessary as breathing" for an academic and an artist. The laziness story was a mere shadow on the wall cast by puppeteers.

Anzaldúa's perception of herself as lazy did not originate with her. She did not write the script she had memorized. A Mexican *jota* (queer woman) who lacks steady employment and insurance, who spends her hours reading and writing, but also sleeping and taking walks on the beach, one who lets her dishes pile up, *is* considered lazy in the broader US context. Anzaldúa was not wrong to think that her mother would buy into the stereotype, nor that other Mexican American mothers would also believe it, nor that many Anglos in the United States would believe it. But as a philosopher, Anzaldúa questioned the stories she had been told, went looking for alternative myths, and created new ways of seeing.

After looking straight at Coatlicue, Anzaldúa realized something about her depression: whatever she hid from herself came out eventually. Without Coatlicue to lay her low, Anzaldúa would never have stopped moving. The pain Coatlicue offered Anzaldúa was excruciating, but Anzaldúa answered it by writing. "If we can make meaning" out of our Coatlicue states, she wrote—and that's a big if—"our greatest disappointments and painful experiences can lead us toward becoming more and more of who we are."[58] Coatlicue offers us a hint of self-knowledge, but only along the path of darkness.

———

At Socrates's hearing, he said that an unexamined life is not worth living. He believed that philosophy can help us know ourselves and live better. For Anzaldúa, depression served a similar function. You need not believe that depression has any inherent positive meaning to see why Anzaldúa would say that Coatlicue helped her see something in the dark. The serpent goddess may lay us down, but she can also help us face what we fear.

Socrates also said that we are pregnant with ideas. His mother was a midwife who helped women give birth to babies. Socrates fancied himself a midwife too, but the kind who helped men give birth to wisdom. Socrates's art, which he called philosophy, was to "prove by every test whether the offspring of a young man's thought is a false phantom, or instinct with life and truth."[59] He tested people by asking them about their idea—teachers sometimes call it "Socratic questioning"—until he could figure out if their baby was strong and healthy; if it was not, he believed that it should be exposed.

Socrates may have been barren (by his own telling), but Anzaldúa was not. With Coatlicue's help, she birthed herself over and over and over (and helped others birth themselves by publishing their essays). She described herself as both mother and baby. She called her experience with Coatlicue a "dry birth," a "breech birth," a "screaming birth," and finally, "one that fights her every inch of the way."[60] By birthing herself anew every time Coatlicue came calling, Anzaldúa gained the ability to become a new person and see things from a new perspective. "When you're in the midst of the Coatlicue state, you're gestating and giving birth to yourself. You're in the womb state."[61]

Anzaldúa did not invent the harmful narrative about lazy Mexicans that was poisoning her. But it was not until she was in the arms of Coatlicue that she could see what was going on. She needed to stop washing dishes to see that the story she had believed was toxic. As much as Anzaldúa resisted Coatlicue, Coatlicue gave her new eyes, and she saw that the lives of Chicana artists and intellectuals are not lazy or selfish.

If Anzaldúa had denied her darkness and run toward the light—if she had tried to stay positive, for example, and to chase away the bad thoughts about herself instead of investigating them—she would probably never have realized that her narrative came from outside her. Without Coatlicue, perhaps Anzaldúa would not have questioned the harm done to many queer, left-handed folk artists and healers who are shamed in similar ways. Knowledge and self-knowledge are not found only in the light but also in the dark, "*en esa cueva oscura*."[62] And although Coatlicue hurt Anzaldúa with her stony embrace, she also offered "inner knowing."[63]

Almost fifteen years after publishing *Borderlands/La Frontera*, Anzaldúa embedded her depressive episodes into a seven-stage process that ended in *conocimiento*, new knowledge and action. She made the Coatlicue state the third stage in this not always linear process. After the emotional earthquake of the diabetes diagnosis hit Anzaldúa at fifty years old, she described feeling torn between the narrative she used to tell about herself—that she'd "paid her dues to pain" and was now ready to "do good work"—and a new, as of yet unknown narrative. This in-betweenness left her at the mercy of Coatlicue, who would arrest her body and mind, leaving her "dysfunctional for weeks."[64]

At last something—she did not name it—would propel her into the fourth stage and encourage her to get out of bed. In the fifth stage—named after Coyolxauhqui, whose body was torn apart and spread all over the Earth—Anzaldúa re-membered herself. Like Coyolxauhqui, Anzaldúa had to put her dismembered pieces back together again, but she found that they didn't go back where they used to be. Whether we suffer from clinical depression or not, we are all dismembered at least once in our lives and will need to re-member ourselves.

In the sixth stage, Anzaldúa reconnected with all of the people she had isolated herself from during the Coatlicue state. In the seventh stage, she engaged in "creative acts" like "writing, art making, dancing, healing, teaching, meditation, and spiritual activism."[65] These acts helped Anzaldúa make meaning of her depression—not because artists need depression to fuel their art, but because depression craves expression.

Instead of hiding her depression in an era when many people did so (especially racial and ethnic minorities), Anzaldúa turned writing about depression into a form of "spiritual activism." She successfully translated a raced and gendered source of shame—"I am lazy"—into creative actions: writing books, giving public talks, and teaching in classrooms. The *dolor* Anzaldúa suffered may have been personal, but the laziness that she had assumed was idiosyncratic to her—the sign of her personal inadequacy—turned out to be a millstone tied to the necks of other oppressed people committed to the life of the mind. "I survived all the racism and oppression by processing it through the writing. It's a way of healing. I put all the positive and negative feelings, emotions, and experiences into the writing, and I try to make sense of them."[66]

Aztec philosophy and mythology enabled Anzaldúa to approach depression as a "complex holism" instead of a simplistic brokenness.[67] Through her new eyes, she saw that she had been touched by a goddess. The Brokenness Story, which says that depression is disease, leaves no room for goddesses. Preferring the moon to the sun distanced Anzaldúa from the light of medicine. It freed her to make up her own nonmedical (not to be confused with anti-medical) narrative about her depression.

———

During the thick of the Covid-19 pandemic, I was invited to be a guest philosopher for a Zoom course, "Philosophy in the Time of Covid," put on by the Ninety-Second Street YMCA in New York City and hosted by my friend and colleague John Kaag. Participants talked about how they were handling the death that was all around them. One participant told us that since he'd already "lost everything" when he lost his wife the previous year, Covid-19 was nothing to him. He said life was too short to hold grudges. I then commented on the tricky business of redemptive suffering—trying to make meaning of something that very well may be meaningless—and I said something about not liking the language of "lessons learned."

In response, the now prickly widower said, "Well, I *do* like the language of lessons learned." When it comes to dark moods that are vilified in the extreme, such as grief and depression, whatever lessons there are to learn can only be learned in the first person. I did not know what it was like to lose a spouse, or how I might respond, because I have not experienced that loss myself. When I share Anzaldúa with my students, I don't tell them how to think or what to believe. I offer them her story of suffering, and the words she used to recolor her struggle, with the hope that they might find her philosophy relatable, relevant, and helpful. Many of my students, especially the ones who are "excruciatingly alive to the world," have taken solace in Anzaldúa's countercultural attitude toward depression.[68] Her willingness to stay on her own side instead of calling herself broken showed us an alternative to "broken and beautiful." Depressed people are not broken. Angry people are not broken. Grieving people are not broken. Anxious people are not broken. Dolorous people are not broken.

My students report learning some lessons from Anzaldúa. These lessons can be tricky because they could almost be romanticizing depression. But if we accept the premise that we cannot eradicate depression while leaving the sufferer intact, then we can think of them as attempts to find a language of cohabitation: how to live with depression without hating yourself.

First, seeing depression by the light of the moon reveals that, although people with depression are not required to tell their stories, it can help. We need not believe that suffering has any redemptive meaning to play it on the piano, write it on the page, or draw it out in the footsteps of a long hike. These acts may or may not help people feel better during the acute phase of a depressive episode (I suspect mostly not), but after getting past the worst of it, self-expression can help. Anzaldúa advocated for "sharing the stress and the skills by connecting with different people through healing therapies and activism."[69] Likewise, as Andrew Solomon wrote in *The Noonday Demon*, "talking about my depression has made it easier to bear the illness and easier to forestall its return. I'd recommend coming out about depression."[70]

Anzaldúa called her creative expression "spiritual activism." Like Unamuno, Anzaldúa thought of her pain as a "conduit" to reach other suffering souls.[71] Likewise, Solomon's masterful study of depression would not be half as compelling if it were simply an investigation into a disease. His words were born of personal anguish; they do not hide, and neither does he. Judging by its status as a best-seller, the book has been a conduit to suffering individuals worldwide. It is spiritual activism in written form, and not the bright-sided variety. Solomon does not thank God for his depression, but he does use it to reach emotional lefties everywhere and to show righties what it is like to live with depression.

But just because Anzaldúa and Solomon used their experiences with depression to some end does not mean that we must. And just because depression can be built into the story of a self does not mean that we should be letting ourselves flounder in the pit of despair. Seeing depression by the light of the moon does not require cutting ourselves off from interventions like medication and therapy, yoga and acupuncture. Anzaldúa's is not a story of Western medicine versus Aztec mythology. It's a story of Plato *and* Prozac. When Anzaldúa craved relief, she considered a variety of healing techniques available to her at the time, including "self-development programs, Alcoholics

Anonymous meetings, self-help books, tapes, therapists, and learning institutions, where we are developing mental/spiritual/emotional healing skills."[72] If her health insurance, which she had only intermittently, had paid for her to see an acupuncturist and get medication, she might have done both.[73]

Solomon, too, explains his willingness to try just about anything. "Depression is an illness of how you feel, and if you feel better, then you are effectively not depressed anymore." If Western medication can cancel out the "nullity" that Solomon speaks of, then it's working. If dancing does, then it's working. No one today has to "tough out" depression, but the fact that we can't eradicate it is no reason not to try alleviating it.

Similarly, when we ask whether a person "needs" to suffer to make art, we are asking the wrong question. The Light Metaphor conveniently fails to tell people that we do not get a choice in many matters of suffering. Sooner or later, we pay the price of living. We cannot avoid experiencing *dolores*, and we cannot choose to turn off our pain: no medicine is that powerful. Our only choice is whether and how to use our pain, and how to build it into the narrative of our lives. Better questions to ask are, *What will I do with my experiences of suffering? What can I see now that I could not see before?*

My students also learn from Anzaldúa that seeing depression by the light of the moon does not require that *zurdos* love their depression any more than Anzaldúa loved her diabetes. She accepted and hated her depression, ending her poem "Healing Wounds" with these words:

Never realizing that to heal
There must be wounds
To repair there must be damage
For light there must be darkness.[74]

Even as Anzaldúa's dishes piled up, she refused to turn against herself. By refusing to interpret her "bleeding and hair pulling" solely as signs of mental or physical brokenness, Anzaldúa saw them as powerful and informative. She referred to her depression as "dwelling in the depth of night consciousness," and she even craved light sometimes (as is natural), but she was unwilling to wholly abandon the darkness for the light.[75] In one email, she would write, "I can't seem to get my spirits up," and in the next she'd add, "It feels like this is where I need to be for now."[76] With Anzaldúa's help, my students can hate their depressive episodes and integrate the fact of their depression into the story of their lives.

Anzaldúa was bilingual, like most of my students. She spoke the languages of dark and light, in both English and Spanish, and she even created new, hybrid Tex-Mex metaphors to explore inner and outer worlds by moonlight. If we can turn either/or thinking (either Anzaldúa's depression was harrowing or it provided an insight) into both/and thinking (Anzaldúa's depression was harrowing and it provided an insight), we can let our many languages and accents bloom.

———

Finally, if the light of the moon suggests that we think of depression as an individual problem instead of a societal affliction, we're half wrong. It's both.

The cases of depression that look most baffling in the light—like Solomon getting depressed after publishing a successful book or fellow author William Styron after winning a prestigious writing award—have been used by psychologists as evidence that some depressions are "without cause."[77] Under the Light Metaphor, which pairs "good things" like success with happiness, depression is mostly befuddling. *If everything is going great for you, why would you get depressed? You must be dysfunctional.*

An Anzaldúa-inspired response would be that if there is ever a time when the pressure on you to be a relentless beam of light gets intense, it is when you publish a book and it wins awards. In other words, a depression that hits you when you are supposed to be happy is most certainly *not* uncaused. In a world where attitudes of gratitude are mandatory, not feeling bright when you have *every reason* to can itself be a factor in depression. So can finishing a project that provided your life with years' worth of meaning or stability. So can an outsized imposter syndrome (which tends to be highly prevalent among—surprise!—minorities).[78] So can a fear that your life has nowhere to go but downhill after such success. When seen in the dark, or by the light of the moon, otherwise baffling cases of depression make much more sense.

Instead of expecting an author to be on cloud nine when they publish a book and win awards, what if we assume that they might soon get depressed? What if we considered depression one of the possible side effects of success? What if we stopped thinking we know what should or should not cause a person's depression? Surely, we would not want to call Anzaldúa's depression uncaused, given her very alienated childhood, her medical conditions, and our racist-sexist-homophobic culture. Who knows how many cases of "uncaused" depression have deep roots like hers, roots that do not appear on the surface or in the light?

As long as mental health talk in our society sounds like happiness literature—equating health with optimism, for example—then those of us who are paying stricter attention to the ills of the world will not be counted as mentally healthy.

Between Covid-19 mutations, political extremism, and reports of child poverty across the globe, we are discontented indeed. If "should" statements are in order, perhaps it would be more reasonable to say that we "should" be unhappy most of the time, and depressed for a good chunk of our adult lives. Through this darker lens, happiness looks like a brazen refusal to empathize with a broken world, and depression looks like an individual manifesting the symptoms of a social illness.

When we attribute depression to a person's brain gone inexplicably awry instead of seeing it as one of the products of a twisted culture's insistence that we whistle while we work ourselves to death, we're ignoring the tools we could be using to criticize the working and living conditions of women, People of Color, and oppressed people of all kinds. The more we ditch society's bright expectations that we should be uniformly happy, busy, and bouncing out of bed every day, and the more we talk about our daily struggles, especially when the world says we are "supposed" to be happy, then the more we will see that there is a home for emotional lefties. There are probably more of us than we think.

What would change in our society if depression went by many names? What if, for example, we all believed in *susto*, Mexican culture's phenomenon of "soul fright"? Anzaldúa describes it in *Borderlands/La Frontera: The New Mestiza* as an affliction that anyone can suffer, and one that has remedies. The understanding about *susto* that is most relevant to depression is that the sufferer "is allowed to rest and recuperate, to withdraw into the underworld without drawing condemnation."[79] What if our society could start by allowing us a solid week in bed without judgment? Could such a shift in perspective—societal, not just personal—change the emotional landscape of our society? Would a depressed person feel less broken if their condition were depicted in our society as routine, or even as a visit from a goddess?

Anzaldúa's ideas liberate by pulling us away from the familiar scripts that have been written for women and wives, for Mexicans and mothers, but her philosophy is not the only way to rethink depression. There are other, equally colorful ways to talk about such an excruciating experience, and it is worth flooding our society with them.

———

When I was young, I played basketball. I was much stronger with my right hand, and in the first two years of high school I played to my strength. Then I quit. I feared I wasn't good enough for the varsity team. In fact, I hadn't taken the time to build up my left arm. The best athletes, dancers, and musicians are those who know how to work from both sides of the court, with both sides, with both hands. For too long, righties have been treated like they have only one hand; the left hand is just a helper. Lefties, on the other hand, have historically been treated as less than human, because their dominant hand is perceived as useless. It wasn't long ago that five-year-old lefties entering school would be forced to write—through constant threat of the ruler—with their right hand. *Zurdos* were seen as broken but fixable beings, and in many ways they still are. Isn't it better for everyone to learn to use both hands?

Andrew Solomon tells a story of visiting a rural village in Bali in which everyone, both deaf and hearing, uses sign language. "What I found when I went into that village," reports Solomon, "was that being deaf really wasn't that much of a disability if you lived in a world where everyone could sign."[80] Our emotional village could use some redesigning in this direction, so that mental illnesses could stop looking like disabilities. If we began to diversify our depression narratives, then we could build a society where emotional lefties felt human instead of fixable. And emotional righties—whether they call themselves optimists, sunny people, or Tiggers—would benefit from learning to use their left hand, to feel and experience their dark moods without being so terrified. They might even find themselves to be ambidextrous.

The aim of this chapter has not been to extol the invisible blessings of depression, but rather to suggest that depression gives us another pair of eyes that, without requiring our gratitude, recolor our world and complicate the stories we tell of our various *dolores*, both as individuals and as a society. Like Anzaldúa, we can strive to be multilingual, speaking the language of Western medicine and Coatlicue and *susto*. We can all help create and live in *el mundo zurdo*.

chapter 5

learning to be anxious

In 2009, anxiety overtook depression as the number-one concern among college students, and in my decade-plus of teaching in the university since then, I have only seen anxiety among these young adults get worse.[1] It used to be that one or two students (out of forty) would disappear during class, then visit my office hours to tell me they suffered from anxiety. But in the last five years, even before the stresses of the Covid pandemic, multiple students have been leaving my classroom multiple times in a seventy-five-minute period. In my initial insecurity, I assumed they were leaving because they couldn't stand my teaching; then my ego countered that idea with the cliché of screen-damaged attention spans. I only gradually realized that anxiety was nudging many of my students to flee. I have gotten more emails and have had more face-to-face conversations than ever with them about social and personal anxiety. Some tell me they are in therapy or on medication, some have sought and been granted formal accommodations by Student Accessibility Services, and others are just beginning to put a name to what they have been feeling since they were six.[2] "I can't look at other people if I sense they're looking at me." "I can't sit in class without my anxiety flaring." "I wish I were invisible." Students have asked for help in securing an appointment at the university's counseling center, only to become so anxious that they could not keep the appointment. As a result of repeated interactions like these, I had to ask: *Why is college student anxiety getting worse?* And also: *Can philosophy help?*

Students like Eva—a philosophy major whose half smile always suggests she's on the brink of a brilliant idea—have reason to be anxious. School shootings have been a reality since the University of Texas Tower Shooting of 1966 in Austin, five hours north of UTRGV. It was the first mass murder on a college campus, before Eva was even born. Over the next fifty years there would be eight more campus shootings in the United States. When Eva was ten, we woke up to a housing crisis and stock market crash, news of which upended kids and adults alike. Eva was seventeen when Donald Trump became president; wherever she falls on the political spectrum, she has been absorbing hateful messages from and/or about him as she has entered adulthood. In 2020 it was Covid-19 that made Eva anxious. She was forced to brace herself for death every time her mother, father, *abuela*, or *tía* left the house, praying she would not be called by the hospital. Because Eva's parents were classified as essential workers, she woke up one morning as the primary caretaker of two younger siblings who would be locked down and attending school remotely for the unforeseeable future. What did not occur to Eva was that her experiences put her in the same existential space as thousands of other students at the university.

When ten students from a single class come into my office one by one to tell me they suffer from anxiety, it hits me that each thinks their anxiety is unusual. They don't know they are sitting next to someone who told me the same thing yesterday. Since breaking confidentiality was never an option, I resolved to talk about anxiety in the classroom more generally until they saw how common it was. Thankfully, in an Existentialism course there is no shortage of opportunities to discuss dark moods. I figured that if the students knew about each other, they would feel less alone. They might even feel less broken.

One day, when the class was discussing the Danish philosopher Søren Kierkegaard's thoughts on anxiety—the subject of this chapter—Eva opened up. She had taken classes with me before, but she still struggled to speak in class. Looking down and occasionally at me, she described her battle with social anxiety. She told the class what she had already told me privately: it was hard for her to attend classes. Samuel, a sophomore philosophy minor who favored striped shirts and called himself a "weirdo," nodded in agreement. He admitted to having recently driven to campus for a class only to find himself unable to get out of his car. More nods. It was working, at least for those students who drove to campus that day and made it all the way to their desks. I was grateful for their willingness to be vulnerable and glad to not be the only one who knew how many of them were suffering in a similar way.

What I had not anticipated from all of these conversations was that the students had something else in common: the ones who felt anxious also felt shame. They felt bad about feeling bad and wished for nothing more than to feel normal. *What about all of the mental illness destigmatization posters I see around campus?* I asked myself. *If anxiety is so common, why do my students still feel so ashamed of it?* It occurred to me that the stories society tells about anxiety may be making college students— and the rest of us—feel worse, not better.

The competing stories floating around about anxiety make it virtually impossible for students like mine to feel okay about feeling bad. Students tell me they have a disorder, an illness, a dysfunction, a chemical imbalance. They are working on it with medication, meditation, gratitude journals, and forest baths. They are trying to fix their anxiety and are willing to seek help, but they only feel worse when they fail to tame their anxious thoughts. Despite their best efforts, the stories my students hear about anxiety have left them feeling shame: feeling bad about feeling anxious. Here is the Brokenness Story at work, and I suspect it's not just college students absorbing the message that anxiety is something to be ashamed of.

The oldest story about anxiety still floating around today is a religious one. The Christian author Max Lucado wrote a book called *Anxious for Nothing*, which equates being anxious with a lack of faith. According to Lucado and many other Christians, anxiety is a sign that you don't trust enough in God's plan. It's a sin in the eyes of God, but it can be redeemed. Believe that God will take care of everything, and your anxiety will subside. With God in control, they say, there is nothing to be anxious about.

The second story of anxiety comes from dead philosophers but lives on through contemporary therapists. The ancient Stoics believed that anxiety amounts to an error in reasoning. If you are anxious, they posited, it is not because you are a sinner. You are anxious because you suffer from disordered beliefs. To feel better, you need to get your crooked thoughts straightened out. As we've seen in earlier chapters, ancient Roman and Greek Stoics believed that we gain control over our feelings by gaining control over our thoughts. Both thoughts and feelings are "up to us," the slave-turned-philosopher Epictetus said, unlike reputation and wealth, which are mostly out of our control. If our feelings are causing us to suffer, we can change them and gain peace of mind.[3] Through a series of lifelong practices (which have been revived in the contemporary world), like writing letters, keeping a journal, rewriting harmful narratives, meditating, talking with friends, and imaginary exposure therapy, a Stoic can retrain her errant feelings to answer to her reason.

This Stoic worldview has been revived and given scientific credibility in cognitive behavioral therapy (CBT), which offers a remarkably similar explanation of anxiety and prescribes similar practices to alleviate suffering. According to the website VeryWellMind, an "award-winning resource for reliable, compassionate, and up-to-date information on the mental health topics that matter most to you,"

> The premise of CBT is that your thoughts—not your current situation—affect how you feel and subsequently behave. So, the goal of CBT is to identify and understand your negative thinking and ineffective behavior patterns and replace them with more realistic thoughts and effective actions and coping mechanisms.[4]

Like the Stoics, cognitive behavioral therapy says that we—not our circumstances—are responsible for our "negative thinking" and "ineffective behavior patterns." If you are anxious, a cognitive behavioral therapist can help you detach from your anxiety by convincing you that your thoughts are self-defeating. Millions of people find this logic empowering, and CBT is now considered the gold standard therapy for anxiety.[5] Cognitive behavioral therapists have helped countless people manage their anxiety, as their philosophical ancestors once did.

Some of my students have tried CBT. They have learned to interpret their anxiety as an error in reasoning. But the overwhelming majority of them are caught up in a different story of their suffering. The story they tell me most often is that there is something chemically wrong with them. Their brains are broken.

The dominant story of anxiety today comes from psychiatrists, who call it a chemical imbalance. Scientists have long since discredited the circa 1990s idea that anxiety is specifically a serotonin deficiency, but it's still widely believed. Of the three stories, chemical imbalance is the one my students tell most often about their anxiety. Neither religious confession nor therapy are going to help, they believe. Only chemicals can fix them.

The idea that anxiety is a medical illness is not new. It's not as though ancient philosophers called anxiety a soul problem and we moderns mucked it up with our brain-scanning machines.[6] In the fifth century BCE, the Greek doctor Hippocrates recounted a case of a man who was terrified of hearing someone play the flute at night. By day this man was okay, but if he heard flute music at night he experienced "masses of terrors."[7] Hippocrates diagnosed this problem as a medical disorder. Likewise, Cicero, the Roman statesman (and somewhat embarrassing Stoic we met in the chapter on grief), also believed that anxiety is more than a bout of "spiritual malaise." He considered it a medical illness with physical manifestations.[8]

The difference between ancient times and now is not that we medicalize anxiety. It's the shrinking pool of doctors considered competent to treat this condition. When Cicero talked about doctors curing souls, he meant philosophers, who prescribed a different kind of medicine: better ways to think and talk about things that upset us. In other words, philosophers were the first therapists: Plato came long before Prozac.

Cicero and other ancients simultaneously believed in the value of physicians. The crucial difference—and what distinguishes ancient from modern ways of thinking—was the ancients' belief that philosophers could help people with physical ailments. We don't believe that. To illustrate: When a friend of mine graduated with his PhD in philosophy, his proud mother went around introducing him as "a doctor." Then, to avoid confusing her friends and acquaintances, she would quickly tack on: ". . . but not the kind that helps people."

When Cicero called upon *lovers of wisdom* (the literal rendering of "philosopher") to heal anxiety, he upset both physicians and philosophers. Doctors like Hippocrates did not want philosophers tinkering with medical problems. (Even Galen, the second-century doctor and philosopher, did not appreciate the Stoic tendency to use medical metaphors, like "illness" and "medicine," to describe philosophical *dolores*.)[9] And philosophers were upset because they did not believe that anxiety was strictly a problem for physicians. Sure, anxiety has physical manifestations, but it's also a disturbance of the mind and/or soul. When the Stoics came up with the "anxiety is disordered thinking" story—the same one used today in CBT—they were making a valiant attempt to snatch anxiety away from physicians before they declared it an exclusively medical issue. The Stoics didn't want to call anxious people diseased, but they did want to help them achieve *ataraxia*: freedom from worry. In the twentieth century, philosophers ceded anxiety to the kinds of doctors "who help people." When souls became brains, philosophers lost their jobs to psychiatrists. As Hippocrates had hoped, anxiety is now seen in its present light as a bona fide medical illness. But the change didn't happen overnight. Philosophers weren't officially forced to stop playing doctor until the twentieth century, thanks to a disagreement between Sigmund Freud and Emil Kraepelin.

Like his Stoic ancestors, Freud believed that the last people who should be treating anxiety were physicians. Freud was trained as a neurologist, but he traded in that specialty for psychology because "in medical school a doctor receives training which is more or less the opposite of what he would need as a preparation for psychoanalysis." More philosopher than physician, Freud believed that there was too much medicalization of psychological conditions like anxiety, and that doctors were being trained to adopt what he considered a "false and detrimental attitude."[10]

In the 1920s, Freud gave anxiety its modern name. Previously, it had gone by *vapors, panaphobia,* and *neurasthenia.* He offered *anxiety neurosis,* among other terms, and attributed the condition to a frustrated libido. Later he tempered that position and linked anxiety to a fear of punishment and abandonment. We feel anxious about losing the love of people in our lives who matter most. Freud's ideas permanently opened two doors, therapy and medicine, the latter of which he would rather have kept closed.

Born in the same year as Freud, Kraepelin was a psychiatrist who believed that mental illnesses can be understood scientifically. Like Hippocrates, he wanted ailments like anxiety to be treated as medical problems and not as theological, philosophical, or even psychological ones. Because of Kraepelin's influence, the priests and philosophers were treated as scientifically backwards and got voted off the island. Every year since then, traditional talk-therapists have lost ground to neurologists and pharmacologists. The pharmaceuticals that started flooding the market in 1955 promised anxious people that drugs could help them feel better—and they would not even have to learn to pronounce *ataraxia.* Doctors of the soul would no longer be consulted on anxious perturbations of the mind. From now on, psychiatrists and pharmaceutical companies would handle it.

By the time the first *Diagnostic and Statistical Manual of Mental Disorders (DSM)* was published by the American Psychiatric Association in 1952, mental illnesses had been more scientized than even Kraepelin could have imagined. Anxiety first appeared in the third edition of the *DSM* in 1980, and by 2005 it was regarded as the "most prevalent form of psychological disturbance."[11] Since Kraepelin, the scientization of anxiety has made it the subject of thousands of scientific studies every year, all of them with a focus on anxiety more chemical and less intuitive, more statistical and less anecdotal.

More priests would have jobs if anxiety were still a sin. Fewer prescriptions would be written if it were still thought of predominantly as a case of "cognitive distortions." When the story is told that anxiety is simply a medical illness, its sufferers become patients in need of medical interventions. The psychiatric story of anxiety is currently winning the storytelling contest, with cognitive behavioral therapists trailing just behind. Sometimes we combine these stories—by taking medicine while also practicing CBT. As with depression, a huge benefit of seeing anxiety as the proper subject of medical manuals like the *DSM* is that the potentially life-saving interventions prescribed there are paid for by medical insurance.

But a risk of painting anxiety solely or exclusively as a mental illness is that anxious people like Eva will be tempted to see their anxiety as closer to schizophrenia, which affects barely 1 percent of the population, rather than as part of the human condition, which affects us all. Medicalizing anxiety might make the anxious feel more alone. The medical light makes the human side of anxiety hard to see and overdiagnosis easy, especially in the context of the financial incentives driving the medical industrial complex.

The curmudgeons among us sometimes get the feeling that the *Diagnostic and Statistical Manual of Mental Disorders* makes medical illnesses out of social maladjustments and legitimate life struggles, including anxiety. We raise our eyebrows, and occasionally our voices, when faced with the requirement of a medical diagnosis to persuade insurance companies to cover the cost of helping people. It doesn't sit well with us that drug companies profit from selling lots of chemicals, whether people are accurately diagnosed or not, and whether their medications help or hurt them. It is simply not plausible, some people think, that all of the one-third of US residents who have been diagnosed with anxiety have broken brains.

Some of us also begin to wonder if the dominant story about anxiety is contributing to the high numbers. If our society told an existential story of anxiety instead of a medical or even a Stoic one, perhaps those numbers would be lower. Maybe what Eva and other anxious people consider "out of proportion" would change if we recognized that much anxiety comes from simply being human, and that anxiety is vital to living well. Maybe our anxiety would not feel so extreme if we were not constantly surrounded by LiveLaughLove prints. Maybe we would all be better at living, laughing, and loving if we were not ordered to do so. Maybe only a small percentage of us have severe, debilitating anxiety disorders, and anxiety for the rest of us is in the mild-to-moderate range. But when the societal expectation of anxiety is set at zero—Keeping Calm and Carrying On 100 percent of the time—then any amount of anxiety feels like too much.

Is there an alternative story about anxiety that might help students like mine feel less ashamed of it?

A Google search for "anxiety and shame" yields a mix of pop psychology blogs, teen magazine essays, and scholarly articles on why anxious people tend to experience high levels of shame. Shame is feeling bad about feeling bad; for the anxious, it's feeling bad about feeling anxious. Many people would agree that shame over anxiety is unnecessary and adds a tragic level of suffering to an already painful situation. As a society, we have not found a good explanation for anxiety shame. We might think it results from a failure to appreciate how common anxiety disorders are. If sufferers could only learn how common their anxiety was, the reasoning goes, they would feel less broken.

MakeItOK.org is one of several large-scale campaigns to reduce or erase the stigma around mental illness. Most of its efforts go into getting people to talk about their mental illness, and the campaign gets a boost when a celebrity comes out about their anxiety or depression. The idea is that publicizing mental illness will lead sick souls to feel less alone and seek healing.

The chemical imbalance story is also part of the destigmatization strategy. The "it's not you, it's your brain" messaging is a desperate attempt to take the blame off the individual. People who tell this story believe that your brain is not chemically imbalanced because you're doing something wrong. (In their story, you are neither a sinner nor a faulty reasoner.) The medical story puts anxiety next to drug and alcohol abuse as diseases whose hosts used to be sinners but are now said to be suffering from a disease. When anxiety becomes an illness, the logic continues, people no longer need to feel ashamed of it. They'll visit a doctor just as if they'd broken a bone.

Helpful as it sounds, the chemical-imbalance story is a flawed destigmatization strategy. First, an unwanted side effect of destigmatizing mental illnesses like anxiety is a tragic intensification of the stigma associated with serious mental illnesses (SMIs) like bipolar disorder and schizophrenia. An unexpected consequence of bringing anxious or depressed people under the "mental illness" umbrella has been how readily they point out that they are not "crazy" like those others.[12]

Second, and perhaps more far-reaching, simply destigmatizing anxiety cannot make anxious people feel dignified. Taking away shame is not the same as convincing someone they have dignity. Even if anxiety were to be fully accepted as a common ailment afflicting the entire US population, anxious people would still be called sick. Anxious people are ashamed of anxiety in part because the Brokenness Story says they're broken. The "brain disease" story of anxiety may make Eva and the rest of us feel less alone. But it cannot make us feel whole, dignified, or human.

The way my students talk about anxiety shame suggests that what bothers them is not that they don't know about each other—even though they don't—but that they cannot see the dignity in their anxiety. Anxiety is more than a broken bone. Notice how the American Psychiatric Association (APA) paints it:

> Anxiety is a normal reaction to stress and can be beneficial in some situations. It can alert us to dangers and help us prepare and pay attention. Anxiety disorders differ from normal feelings of nervousness or anxiousness, and involve excessive fear or anxiety. Anxiety disorders are the most common of mental disorders and affect nearly 30 percent of adults at some point in their lives. But anxiety disorders are treatable and a number of effective treatments are available. Treatment helps most people lead normal productive lives.[13]

The major note in this description of anxiety is not that anxiety is normal or beneficial, but that treatment exists. The APA is explicitly trying to reassure individuals that they stand a chance of leading normal and productive lives, but its implicit message is that they are currently not doing so. Eva felt ashamed of her anxiety, just as C. S. Lewis felt ashamed of his grief and Jody felt ashamed of her *dolor*. The APA may insist that anxiety can be "normal" and "beneficial," but the quicker it goes into talk about treatment, the quicker the jig is up. The distinction between "normal" and "disordered" anxiety buckles once it says that 30 percent of us have an anxiety disorder. One in three may not constitute a majority, but it seems awfully close to normal.

Shame over anxiety gets even more complicated when we hear the medical story overlaid by the Stoic/cognitive behavioral therapy story. While the medical story centers on brains and chemicals, the Stoic/CBT story locates the problem in the anxious person's "negative thinking" and "ineffective behavior patterns." CBT's goal, remember, is to dispel negative thoughts and behaviors and "replace them with more realistic thoughts and effective actions and coping mechanisms."[14] So are anxious people broken or irrational? Or both?

The Stoic/CBT story says we are responsible for holding on to our harmful thoughts, including anxiety. It's tempting to believe that happiness is a matter of personal choice. This belief has propped up thousands of self-help books since the 1950s. The good thing is that it often works: countless anxious people have been helped by cognitive behavioral therapy. They have changed their damaging thought patterns and have felt less anxious as a result. Their success in fitting better into a world that has no tolerance for anxiety is significant, and I do not want to negate it.

But when CBT does not work, watch out. The blame lands squarely on the sufferer—as it did with Hayden Shelby, who believed that cognitive behavioral therapy could help her "kick" her "negative thought patterns." Shelby published her experience with CBT in *Slate* magazine. "The cumulative message I've gotten about CBT," Shelby reports, amounted to: "It's effective, so it should work, and if it doesn't work, it's because you didn't try hard enough."[15] As helpful as CBT has been for many people, it's guilty, like well-intentioned self-help books, of putting an awful lot of pressure on us to get ourselves out of our misery. In trying to empower us, the ancient Stoic theory that drives cognitive behavioral therapy—we control our feelings by controlling our thoughts—makes us responsible for our negative moods. Put the other way around, CBT leaves the anxiety-producing features of the world unchallenged, just as happens with therapeutic strategies for handling anger. The going assumption is that the studs keeping the hallways of our existence narrow are fixed. All we can do is put the emotional squeeze on ourselves to fit into a world that won't tolerate anxiety.

We're even responsible for bootstrapping ourselves out of shame. Scientists and self-help books agree that shame is bad for our health. The good news, they inform us, is that we can get better by cutting out negative self-talk. "Be kinder to yourself." "Talk to yourself as you would talk to a friend." "You need not be ashamed." By these lights, even the shame we feel over anxiety is something we do to ourselves and can stop doing. If we want to stop feeling ashamed, we can go to therapy or read *What to Say When You Talk to Yourself*.

Imagine telling a bulimic that she can stop telling herself a toxic story about desirable and undesirable bodies. If she would only agree to change her thinking, she would not feel the need to purge. This implies that the best solution for each of the millions of girls and women (and boys, in increasingly alarming numbers) telling themselves the same toxic stories about desirable and undesirable bodies is to seek therapy, one by one. This approach ignores the question of whether millions of bulimics are telling themselves these stories or simply reading the writing on the cave wall.

At least we have gotten wise to the idea that shame over body image is a social and not simply an individual phenomenon when it comes to eating disorders. The term "body-shaming" has opened a helpful discussion about shame, one that is promising for discussions about anxiety and other mental illnesses. "Body-shaming" refuses both the recommendation that the bulimic's problem be treated as an individual one and the idea that her shame is self-caused. Instead, the term blames society for inundating young people with toxic messages about desirable bodies.

Could we speak similarly about anxiety-shaming? Anxious people did not make up the idea that anxiety is disordered. They did not decide to feel ashamed of it out of nowhere, any more than they came to feel their anxiety out of nowhere. On top of treating shame as self-caused, the Stoic/CBT story also describes shame as an individual problem. Anxious people absorb the message that their anxiety is treatable and that it's their job to seek help, so how can they be blamed for feeling both diseased and responsible? The idea that we can and should stop shaming ourselves, and that we can and should stop feeling anxious, is a shadow—the same shadow thrown by self-help books when they tell us we make our own happiness.

Yes, cognitive behavioral therapy (often) works. Humans have an amazing capacity to change their thinking, and we can do it one by one, each anxious person seeking individual therapy. But at what cost when we blame the prisoner who dutifully reads the shadows on the wall instead of searching for the throng of puppeteers who are throwing them? Instead of urging people to come in for treatment, for example, the thought leaders of our society could at least investigate the idea that one reason anxiety shame even exists is that anxiety is (almost) never publicly portrayed as a type of intelligence.[16]

Anxiety is painful, mostly unpleasant, and sometimes debilitating. But the last thing anxious people need is to feel shame on top of feeling anxious. As long as anxiety is equated with brokenness, it will be accompanied by anxiety shame. Eva did not shame herself. She's been staring at a shadow that depicts anxiety as dysfunction. It's insulting to tell her—even if it's true!—that she can always close her eyes.

Those telling the story of anxiety today are inadvertently promoting the Light Metaphor. They are captivated by shadows they have mistaken for truth. It is not a lie that anxiety can be debilitating, and it's not *unhelpful* that anxiety has become the subject of a public discourse. Since the pandemic, my students talk much more freely about their mental health diagnoses in general. But the blunt fact remains that, in a world where any amount of anxiety is deemed dysfunctional, we're going to have a whole lot of Evas who feel both anxious and ashamed.

The Brokenness Story is hurting us—and feeding our anxiety in the process. Is there no other way of looking at anxiety than as illness? What we need beyond more destigmatization campaigns is a fuller story about anxiety, one that uplifts the spirit rather than a story that degrades it, one that keeps us from turning against ourselves. We can do better than "you are not alone."

Søren Kierkegaard's analysis of anxiety does better. It dignifies anxiety without minimizing the suffering it causes. And although, from his Christian viewpoint, Kierkegaard ultimately believed that faith is what truly helps us learn from our anxiety, non-Christians and Christians alike can take from him the powerful message that we should turn toward our anxiety rather than away from it.

———

When Kierkegaard was twenty-seven, he fell in love with Regine Olsen, the fourteen-year-old girl he would love until death did him part. Three years later he proposed, and she accepted. A year after that, though, he broke their engagement and her heart. She begged him to reconsider. Her father begged him. No dice. Søren would not surrender.

For almost two hundred years, Kierkegaard fanatics worldwide have asked themselves why Søren would not marry Regine, the woman who once received a letter from him declaring that if he were granted seven wishes, he would wish the same thing seven times:

> That neither Death, nor Life, nor Angels, nor Principalities, nor Powers, nor the present, nor that which is to come, nor the Exalted, nor the Profound, nor any other creature may tear me from you, or you from me.[17]

Why did he tear himself away from Regine? Kierkegaard blamed his decision on "congenital" anxiety, which he said he felt even in the womb. Søren could not remember a time before anxiety, and he pitiably asked himself in his diary why he failed to "thrive as other children do." "Why was I not wrapped around in joy, why did I come to look into that region of sighs so early?"[18] Søren never got to be a carefree kid, or even a wild child like Audre Lorde. Like some of us who feel off the spectrum of the normal, he was asking, *Why me? Why am I so different from everyone else?*

Across sixteen books and twelve volumes of journals numbering thousands of pages, Kierkegaard's mention of being anxious as a fetus was the most he ever wrote about his mother. Ane Lund had been the Kierkegaards' housemaid before becoming Mrs. Michael Pedersen Kierkegaard. Michael's first wife had died tragically and left him no children, but Ane bore him seven babies, with little Søren coming last. Their home was not a happy place. Søren's mother and five of his siblings had died by the time he was twenty-one, leaving his father drowning in sorrow and blaming himself.[19] God, he reasoned, was taking revenge on a starving little Jutland boy who had raised his fist against Him all those years ago. Michael had been destitute, and in a desperate act he cursed God. But instead of smiting little Michael right there and then, God sent him to Copenhagen and made him one of the richest men in Denmark. Michael never forgot his curse, and he felt certain that, just when he got used to having plenty, his vengeful God set to work, snatching wives and children from him one by one, in payback for what he did years earlier as a boy.

In the wreckage, Peter (the "upright son") and Søren ("a bright fellow gone to ruin"), were left alone with their tormented but still deeply religious father.[20] When Søren was twenty-five, his father died, leaving Søren a large inheritance. His plan was to be a self-published author and then to die by thirty-four like his siblings and Christ. Little did Søren know that he would make it all the way to forty-two, when his anxiety would focus on whether he had enough money to pay his hospital bill.

Kierkegaard's anxiety was largely religious. In one of his pseudonymous books, Kierkegaard tells the story of a father who shows a series of images to his child. One image shows Napoleon looking majestic. Another shows William Tell about to shoot the apple off of his son's precious head. The third, "deliberately placed among the others," shows Jesus Christ crucified.

> The child will not immediately, not even quite simply, understand this picture; he will ask what it means, why is he hanging on such a tree. Then you explain to the child that it is a cross and that to hang upon it means to be crucified, and that crucifixion in that country was the most painful death penalty.[21]

This episode may very well have happened to little Søren, since we know that his father's Christianity stressed Christ's suffering more than his joy. It made the child anxious, Kierkegaard wrote, "and afraid for his parents, the world, and himself."[22] Michael Pedersen's life had always been shaded by a "dark background," which Søren inherited along with his fortune. "The anxiety with which my father filled my soul," Kierkegaard wrote in his diary, was passed from father to son, as was "his own frightful depression, a lot of which I cannot even write down."[23]

In response to his father's melancholy, Kierkegaard "acquired an anxiety about Christianity and yet felt powerfully attracted to it."[24] As it does for many people, Christianity triggered Kierkegaard's anxiety (and may have been partly responsible for his father's melancholy). Love also made Kierkegaard anxious.

Soon after he decided to abort his engagement, Kierkegaard decided that he would rather Regine marry someone else than love someone plagued by anxiety. He planned to make all of Copenhagen think he was a cad who had seduced and then discarded Regine. That way, she and her family could hold on to their dignity at Kierkegaard's expense. But it would also mean that Regine herself might believe it. "I am still plagued by anxiety," he wrote in his journal. He worried: "Suppose that she really begins to believe that I am a deceiver."[25] Kierkegaard didn't like the idea that Regine, believing that he had been false, would hate him. But neither could he stomach the prospect of her finding out that his trickery was motivated by love. If she found out that he had canceled the engagement because he considered his sorrow unfit to share with another human being, she would see him as a quixotic hero instead of a player and might never give up on him.

We'll never find out what Regine believed. She married someone else and moved away from Denmark. But we do know that Kierkegaard remained a bachelor, living all his life with anxiety, despair, and an empty cupboard. Regine had begged Søren to let her live in a cupboard in his living room, so that she could be close to him without interfering with his work. After the break was final, Kierkegaard commissioned a Regine-sized cupboard to be made in her honor. It is among the few of his tragic possessions on display in the Kierkegaard museum in Copenhagen.

Kierkegaard wrote multiple pseudonymous books that touched upon the Regine romance. Some portray him as guilty of deceiving her, and some make him out to be an anxious depressive who loved her faithfully. He sent Regine some of these books and a letter, but the unopened bundle was promptly returned by her husband. One of the books was *The Concept of Anxiety*.

Congenitally anxious little Søren was born to become Virgilius Haufniensis ("The Watchman of the Harbor"), the pseudonymous author of *The Concept of Anxiety*.[26] Haufniensis kept vigil over Copenhagen like an anxious mom who stays awake so her kids can rest. Published in 1844, three years after he broke off the engagement, Kierkegaard's book offers a groundbreaking and compelling analysis of anxiety. And even if, like C. S. Lewis, Kierkegaard couldn't quite believe his own positive analysis of anxiety, we can. As a teacher, I guessed that his dark and tragic story stood a better chance of helping my anxious students than the lights of psychology and psychiatry. First, the "melancholy Dane's" analysis of anxiety is not born of light. Second, it makes no promises about getting back to normal.

———

I do not talk about anxiety on the first day of Existentialism class. Instead, I ask the students whether they would take a little purple pill that guaranteed them a pain-free life. A handful of them say no; they would not want to trade in the ugly parts of life—the pain and fear—just for the good bits. They want high highs and low lows, and they are not interested in artificial happiness. At least some of them, however, say yes, reasoning that they would love to be more adventurous, take more risks, and enjoy life more. Pain and fear hold them back from living, they say. It would be much easier to live without them.

What the yesses don't realize is that not feeling pain and not feeling fear are two of the most dangerous afflictions a human can suffer. Congenital analgesia is the inability to form the proper channels between the site of injury and your brain. It stops a person from knowing to remove their hand from a hot burner. Urbach-Wiethe disease indicates damage to the amygdala, the part of our brain that feels fear. In the 1980s, researchers wrote about patient SM-046, whose lack of fear made her vulnerable to physical abuse by strangers and loved ones many times throughout her life.[27]

Both medical conditions make the ability to feel pain and fear look like superpowers by comparison. The same is true for our ability to feel anxious. Socrates told people that a small voice accompanied him everywhere; he called it his *daimon*, and it would warn him if what he was about to do was dangerous or unethical. Maybe anxiety is our *daimon*.

Kierkegaard rejected the idea that anxiety is an imperfection, going so far as to call rejecting anxiety "straightlaced cowardice." He wrote: "The greatness of anxiety is the very prophet of the miracle of perfection."[28] If perfection is a miracle we strive for but can never reach, then it is anxiety that tells us how to get closer to it. It's the voice that warns us about real but uncertain danger. "*Wrong way!*" anxiety says. "*Don't go into that room!*" A person's inability to become anxious is just as dangerous as an inability to feel fear or pain. Only animals and angels don't get anxious, Kierkegaard said (though today we might ask how he's so sure).[29]

His point was that it's better to suffer from anxiety than not to experience anxiety at all. Far from being a medical illness, Kierkegaard believed, anxiety is a uniquely human strength. However often it misguides us, anxiety is a kind of intelligence that is always right . . . about something. (Anxiety's misguidance may be its worst feature.) According to Kierkegaard's model, it's not 30 percent of Americans who are anxious. It's 100 percent of humans. Even if we do not want to model our lives after poor Kierkegaard—who often couldn't practice what he preached—we can start with the idea that anxiety is thoroughly human.

Kierkegaard named anxiety "the infinite possibility of being able."[30] It's what we feel whenever we're faced with a choice. Not knowing what any given choice may lead to can be nerve-wracking. And thrilling, added Kierkegaard.

Kids provide a good example of the thrilling kind of anxiety. The *New York Times* might have recently reported that "toddlers are not immune" from anxiety, but Kierkegaard beat the *Times* to that conclusion by almost two hundred years.[31] In Danish, the word *angest* translates to both "angst" and "dread." It contains an element of energy, but less than the Spanish *ansioso*, which means "eager" or "excited about," compared to the English "anxiety," which skews strictly negative these days. The Danish, like the Spanish, capture the fear of anxiety as well as some of the thrill.

When my son was five, he used to giggle when he did something wrong. At the time I thought he was being sassy, but I came to understand that giggling was his anxiety talking. When he was eight, he told me he loved to "be in a hurry." His heart would race at the prospect of almost being late for something. I told him his feeling was called anxiety, and it can be fun. It can also be stressful. Often it's both. But when we paint anxiety singly—as only painful, difficult, or undesirable—it's hard to redeem it.[32] As long as we're not seeing anything life-giving in anxiety, we're looking at shadows and half-truths.

Kierkegaard believed that we become anxious in the face of possibilities, and that it increases when our possibilities include transgression.[33] Students who cheat on an exam or a significant other are more anxious than those who don't cheat, in Kierkegaard's story, even if they don't show it. The "prohibition awakens in [them] freedom's possibility."[34] My students are right to be anxious, and so are the rest of us. Whether you are a kid, a cheater, or just a regular human being on a Tuesday, realizing you can mess up ratchets up your level of anxiety.[35]

This human condition—living with the knowledge that we can mess up our own lives—is called freedom, which my students think is a good thing before they read Existentialists like

Kierkegaard. They've grown up thinking that freedom is as wonderful as anxiety is terrible. My goal is to interrupt both sets of assumptions and to reverse them until we can all agree that freedom is also terrifying, and that anxiety is also vivifying.

———

If you ask someone on the street whether they would choose to be free or unfree, they would probably choose to be free. My students do. To be free is to be able to take a vacation, quit a job, or back out of a wedding. But if you ask that same person if they want to be responsible for how their life turns out after taking a vacation, quitting a job, or backing out of a wedding, they might waver. Freedom always includes the freedom to mess up.

Philosophically speaking, one of the most anxiety-ridden pieces of advice people give us is, "You can do anything you set your mind to." Try telling that to a college student who doesn't know what they want to do in life and see what happens. Try telling it to a woman who has just left her husband and is experiencing a dizzying freedom. "Anything" is why we're anxious, even if it sounds promising at first. Anxious people can immediately sniff out the negative configuration of happy-sounding buzzwords. "Anything is possible" means that my family can fall apart, that a student can bring a gun to class and kill me, or that a bomb can go off in the subway. What riddles us with anxiety is the "anything" in being able to do "anything in the world" when that world is a place where anything can happen. If you have ever anxiously waited for a loved one to get home in the middle of the night, you have experienced the sleeplessness of "anything is possible."

Kierkegaard called anxiety the "dizziness of freedom."[36] He gave us the image of a lonely person looking over an abyss, fists clenched. Even as we learn "to adult," to hold ourselves erect and make our own choices, we are nothing more than wobbly creatures looking everywhere but down. Contemporary psychologists call it "drift" when we choose something halfheartedly. Going to college, getting married, having children—these all look like choices from the outside, but we often embark on them without giving enough consideration to the alternatives. We often choose to do what is expected of us because not choosing to do so would be much harder than meeting those expectations. Drift is a choice we make behind our own backs. We're choosing without really choosing—like my nursing majors who cannot stand the sight of blood but who don't want to disappoint their parents.

After the French Existentialist Jean-Paul Sartre read Kierkegaard's description of anxiety as the dizziness of freedom, he added that looking down into the abyss can make a person nauseated and give them a sense of vertigo. Looking into the abyss is the bad feeling you get when you realize you are radically free to ruin your life. We know deep down that we are responsible for most of what we do, both the choices we make deliberately and the ones we drift into. There is surprisingly little that is completely out of our hands, said Sartre.

For Kierkegaard, Sartre, and the other Existentialists, we cannot live honestly—because we cannot live intentionally—without getting dizzy in the face of decisions. The abyss beckons us to look down, to face the possibility of our utter failure. Regret waits for us in the future as we calmly scroll through Instagram photos to pass the time. Closing our eyes to a decision cannot protect us from the "Why didn't I?" that is to come.[37] Freedom is dizzying. It's wonderful and miserable, and most of all it's expensive. The price of freedom is anxiety.

In an effort to steady ourselves, Sartre observed that humans will sometimes overidentify with their roles. We lean into "mother," "CEO," "student," as though these fixed identities can keep us from falling into the pit of despair. But there are no mothers, CEOs, or students, according to Sartre's logic. There are no introverts, schizophrenics, or Aspies either. We're just anxious humans whose dizziness makes us desperate to tether ourselves to something fixed. The alternative is free-falling, which makes chaining ourselves down at the wrists and ankles—to each other, to jobs we don't like, to children—look pretty good.

But then we wake up in chains. Sartre thinks we're all bundles of disavowed decisions on legs. The *pièce de résistance* of anxiety is the "midlife crisis"—the point at which we ask ourselves how we got here, or why we didn't choose a better life, or what we're going to do with the rest of it.

We make fun of the midlife crisis, notorious for ruining marriages and selling sportscars, but in fact a midlife crisis is our anxiety giving us a second chance. It reminds us that we are not robots or plants. (We are spirit, not just flesh, says Kierkegaard.) We want to live well, to be decent, to be happy. Without anxiety, we would hear no wake-up call, gain no awareness that we have forfeited our freedom. Anxiety gives us access to a part of ourselves that floats above the physical body. Sartre named it our "transcendence," and it's rooting for us to wake up. Without anxiety, we would never wake up. We would not love or live intentionally.

No one I know likes to feel nauseated, but nausea doesn't mean we're broken. It means we're alive. Wobbly though we may be, we are full human beings. A pregnant woman may get nauseous in the first trimester as the creature inside plants its flag on her uterus. Similarly, our *daimon* anxiety plants its flag on our stomachs and makes us weak. In Kierkegaard's story, it's partly our awareness of freedom, choice, and consequence that makes us gloriously, fitfully human. It's an "even better teacher than reality," said the Existential therapist Rollo May, channeling Kierkegaard.[38]

By the end of the Existentialism course, none of the students still believe that a person who does not feel pain, fear, or anxiety is better off than one who does. They take seriously Kierkegaard's suggestion that anxious people are more than a toxic blend of chemicals to be eradicated *"mit Pulver und mit Pillen"* (with powder and with pills).[39] They have come to see that if we try to get rid of anxiety, we would also be getting rid of freedom, sensitivity, perceptiveness, empathy, and a sense of good living. We would be blunting the part of us that is "excruciatingly alive to the world."[40]

Rather than aiming to eradicate anxiety, Kierkegaard offers another option: we can listen to anxiety and approach it as an ally, as a reminder that we are free. Nondebilitating levels of anxiety are a painful part of the human condition, but they are also the prerequisite for an interior life. Even as they start to get that, however, my students still think anxiety is a kind of fear.

―――――

If you have a fear of flying, your therapist can show you statistics suggesting that you should be more scared of getting into a car than an airplane. They can teach you breathing exercises designed to keep you calm during turbulence. They can accompany you on a short flight and talk you through your feelings. But what if your fear of flying is not fear at all? What if it's anxiety about turbulence? About not knowing if it will happen, or when, or for how long? What if turbulence itself is a metaphor for being out of control? And what if being out of control has to do with not knowing when or how you will die? How do you conquer that?

Anxiety cannot be tamed, thought Kierkegaard. At any moment I could get cancer or Covid-19. My kids could get abducted or killed crossing the street. Worse, some combination of these things could happen in the same year. Anxiety is amorphous, and we often mistake it for fear. Unlike fear, anxiety names a bundle of nonspecific ills. It is a voice telling us that things in general are not okay. Anxiety suspects that danger is lurking but cannot describe what it is, where it is, or even when it will surface.

The suspense in a horror movie triggers anxiety in us. The most disturbing movies keep us waiting for hours before giving the killer a face, and sometimes they never do. It's not until we can see the villain that anxiety can successfully turn into fear, which is far easier to cope with than anxiety. Fear has a face. Anxiety has none. Amorphous villains can keep us anxious long after the movie ends. If we were only afraid of the particular serial killer in the movie, our fear would dissipate soon after the credits roll. If our fear is extended to all serial killers, we might continue to be afraid of serial killers but would calm ourselves with statistics about how few people are murdered each year by them. But if the movie triggers thoughts like *anyone could be a killer, anything could happen,* and *I could die!,* then we lose control of our fear, because it's no longer fear that we're experiencing. It's anxiety.

Pandemics like Covid-19 are hotbeds of anxiety. First, the virus is invisible. You cannot see it, which is terrifying enough, but for months we also had no idea where it came from. We disinfected our mail and our groceries. We cleaned surfaces multiple times a day. We did not touch our faces, and we washed our hands for twenty Mississippi seconds every hour. We took off our clothes and showered when we got home. We wore masks with coffee filters in them and prayed that N95s would be made available to the public. Overnight the world became a minefield, so we learned to step lightly and keep watch. The video that went viral comparing Covid-19 to glitter did not help.

If you asked Kierkegaard, he would say that our Covid anxiety was over "nothing," meaning no-tangible-thing. Because we did not know how it was transmitted, and because the virus is invisible to the human eye, our Covid anxiety was more like a pervasive feeling or idea: a stand-in for death, or loss of control, or both. Little droplets of doom seemed to be floating all around us, waiting for us to breathe them in. We named the object of our anxiety "Coronavirus," but we could have just called it "death."

Giving the object of our anxiety a name is a way of trying to turn anxiety into fear. Giving it a face is even more effective. I recall a nightmare in which I was trapped in a large outdoor carnival-type space with hundreds of people. We could not leave, but we all knew there was a man going around killing people one by one. I watched him from my hiding place and waited for my turn. In my sleep, my psyche had mercifully given Covid-19 a human face and, by stoking fear, given my anxiety a night off.

In those early days, we saw people dying by the thousands. We might have said we were afraid of Covid-19 like some people say they are afraid of flying, but Kierkegaard would counter that that feeling we had would have been better termed "anxiety" than "fear."

A lot of Existentialists believe that anxiety is always secretly about death, literally or metaphorically. I may think I am scared of bees, serial killers, and heights, but in reality, Kierkegaard and Sartre would say, I am anxious about dying. Death is the ultimate state of being out of control.[41] It's logical that we would try to tie an amorphous anxiety about death to an object, like a spider or an airplane or even a virus. Doing so focuses our attention on avoiding the spider or the airplane or the virus. To say that anxiety is about death is another way of saying that anxiety is about control: as much as we're anxious about messing up, we're also anxious about the prospect of not being able to choose. Our incessant hand-washing was a way of telling ourselves that we could always do something to keep ourselves from dying. But anxiety always reminds us that it's just not true. Not in the long run.

The Covid-19 pandemic—and the anxiety it caused—raised our awareness of our mortality. Our lives became saturated with meaning in a matter of weeks, or even days. We quit jobs or moved. We played with our kids or doom-scrolled. We took walks or stayed in our homes, turning them into bunkers. We wanted to stay alive, but we all went about it differently, some of us seeking life anew and some renewing our commitment to control.

One of the most interesting aspects of watching anxiety rise during the pandemic for me, an Existentialist philosopher, was the extent to which perfectly healthy people were derailed by it. Colleagues who had no children, no aging parents to take care of, and no underlying medical conditions refused to enter a grocery store for more than a year, relying exclusively on curbside pickup. I noticed that young and healthy people, the ones who had never faced death before, were the ones who became the most anxious and insulated. Unlike my low-income students who had already seen and felt the effects of everyday killers like diabetes, heart disease, and obesity, exacerbated by a lack of health insurance, it had not yet fully sunk in for many of my well-to-do colleagues that sooner or later young and healthy people will die and rot just like everybody else. Covid-19 made a new group of people confront a reality they had been denying.

Predictably, though, when these same people got vaccinated and soon perceived themselves to be out of danger, they went back to the grocery store. Besides a small number of people who remained cautious and kept wearing masks even outside, my well-to-do friends traveled and started eating in restaurants. Armed with the privilege of moderate wealth and jobs they could work from home, they resumed their productive lives, as the *Diagnostic and Statistical Manual of Mental Disorders* hopes we all will when we learn to manage our anxiety. In our society, "getting back to normal" is good.

Not so for the Existentialists. Martin Heidegger—whose *Being and Time* was influenced by Kierkegaard and in turn influenced Sartre—called getting back to normal "flight from death." He would say that those anxious days at the beginning of the pandemic were the closest my colleagues had ever come to living authentically, because it was a time when they made their decisions with their mortality in mind. In those days, we could not escape the fact that we are not ultimately in control. Getting "back to normal," for the Existentialists, means pretending, again and again and again, that we are immune to death, that we can wash our hands and avoid the disease.

For good or bad, anxiety invites us into what Brené Brown calls "the arena" (after Teddy Roosevelt's famous speech), the place where risking, fighting, and dying happen. Anxiety reminds us that we are free and that all manner of things can happen without our consent. But if we sedate our anxiety, what will induce us to climb into the arena, to risk and fight and die?

At the very same time, anxiety is doing some of us serious damage, paralyzing our everyday lives. Is there a way to adopt a harmonious relationship with so irritating a teacher as anxiety?

———

Whenever they move, my parents disable the fire alarms all over their new house, alarms that were installed to save their lives. They do it because they cannot stand the chirping that happens at 4:00 AM every couple of years when the batteries die. No matter how tempting, it's a bad idea to permanently disable a fire alarm, even if it is occasionally prone to misbehaving. Rather than unplug an alarm, it would be better to make sure it's not detecting a fire we cannot yet smell, or one that is burning next door.

Maybe anxiety is a fire alarm that goes off when something isn't right. Fire alarms occasionally misfire, so we cannot always rely on them to tell us if there is a fire or not. But the upside to the metaphor is that anxious people come out looking like we are in tune with the dangers of the world compared to those who sleep soundly underneath disabled fire alarms, always believing they are safe.

People ask, "Why are kids more anxious than ever these days?," but the answer is obvious: "Wake up and look around! Why wouldn't they be more anxious than ever?" The anxious are right to be anxious. Thanks to the internet and a host of other mixed blessings, we have reasons to worry. Given what we ingest daily of pandemics, terrorist attacks, violence (including toward and by the police), war, school shootings, poverty, and the degradation of the environment, anxiety is a legitimate response. Anxiety admits to not knowing what hides around the corner, whether it's good or bad (but suspecting it's mostly bad). The anxious person adroitly recognizes the array of terrifying possibilities in front of us all and responds appropriately: with weak knees and a knotted stomach.

Anxiety is a logical reaction to a terrifying age in which people are nevertheless expected to be grounded, happy, flourishing. Posters instructing us to KEEP CALM AND CARRY ON are pinned over the walls of society, which themselves read: ATTENTION: THIS IS NOT A DRILL. Why would we need a sign telling us IF YOU SEE SOMETHING SAY SOMETHING if nothing is wrong? Our society's busy efforts to cover up the tragic features of life—*nothing to see here!*—actually cause our anxiety to perk up. Voices distract us with incoherent phrases like "Positive Thoughts Create a Positive World." But over this racket, our anxiety shouts about how very doubtful it is that pain, suffering, and death befall us according to our attitude. Clinically anxious people seem to be living in a thriller while the other 70 percent walk around like they're in a rom-com. Who is right? Who is sick?

Looking at them through a Kierkegaardian lens, we should be worried about non-anxious people. How is anyone sleeping soundly in this day and age? What is wrong with them? I know—they must be broken! The Light Metaphor, however, would never allow us to come to this conclusion. Declaring non-anxious people the broken ones is way too dark. Besides, we're already convinced that the anxious people are the broken ones.

If Kierkegaard is right that anxiety is something without which we lose touch with possibility, sensitivity, perceptivity, humanity, and freedom, then how should we feel about it? What should we do about our anxiety? My students tend to like Kierkegaard's idea that anxiety is not an imperfection but rather a sign of intelligence, but they don't know where that leaves therapy and medicine. Should we be getting treated for anxiety even though it's our sixth sense, just because we cannot stand what it is trying to show us? Do we really wish to become sound sleepers?

The kind of therapy we choose to help us with our anxiety will determine which way we go. A therapy that approaches anxiety as an illness and a therapy that approaches it as a teacher will naturally set different goals.

Because cognitive behavioral therapists are (inadvertently) influenced by the light of ancient Stoicism, they define anxiety disorder as a treatable condition. Anxiety is seen as an obstacle instead of a messenger. If I tell myself: "Everyone I love will die, leaving me all alone," a CBT practitioner might ask: "How can you get this harmful thought pattern to change?"[42] In trying to minimize my anxious thoughts, this therapist takes for granted that, because these thoughts make my life more difficult, they are undesirable, even though it's a basic fact that everyone I love will die.

In contrast, Existential psychotherapy isn't focused on disabling the fire alarm. It is based on the ideas of Freud, Jung, Sartre, Nietzsche, and other Existentialists, all of whom agree with Kierkegaard that we should treat anxiety as a teacher or a form of intelligence. The last remaining Existential psychotherapists are more likely to consider anxiety legitimate until proven otherwise. Their aim won't be to minimize it, but to use it to see how you might make changes that enable you to live a more intentional and meaningful life.

An Existential therapist might start with a question like: "How do you want to live?" If they believe that we spend most of our time trying not to ask life's toughest questions, that we'd rather pretend that death is not about to land in our town and leave bodies strewn about, then they're more likely to encourage us to go there.

An Existential therapist would agree with Kierkegaard that humans' anxiety is more than maladaptive thought patterns or chemical imbalances. We are deeply spiritual beings concerned with what the Existentialist psychotherapist Irvin Yalom calls the "big four": death, isolation, meaning in life, and freedom.[43] Investigating our anxiety with an eye to these topics (even when they are disguised as fears) can help us detect what needs changing in our lives.

Could we ever bring ourselves to believe, along with Yalom, that "adults who are racked with death anxiety are not odd birds who have contracted some exotic disease"? Could we begin to think of ourselves as people "whose family and culture have failed to knit the proper protective clothing for them to withstand the chill of mortality"?[44] We all need protective clothing, and the only question is where we will get it from. Some try to get it from illegal drugs, some from family, some from food or wine, and some from posters and mugs. What is the best way to withstand the chill of mortality, given that mortality is a given and will always be chilly?

———

The best-selling author Glennon Doyle suffers from an anxiety so fierce that she turned to food and alcohol abuse just to stay afloat in such a hostile world. Thinking she was broken because she was born sensitive to the ills she saw everywhere, she found a way to unplug all of the fire alarms: never be sober. Drunkenness was the best solution Doyle could come up with to ease her anxiety in a heartbreaking world.

We do not have to go that route (especially if everyone could just shove over and let those of us who are "excruciatingly alive to the world" express ourselves without being told we are too sensitive).[45] We can protect ourselves from the chill of death in healthy, safe, and non-addictive ways. We can learn to knit hats and scarves. We will never start knitting, though, if we refuse to acknowledge that it's getting chillier out. We need to get comfortable looking at the reality of misery and death, even if everyone else is staring at a shadow on the wall.

Doyle reports that, in recovery, a fellow addict gave her a lens through which to see her future life without the protection of alcohol. Being fully human, this wise woman said, "is not about feeling happy, it's about feeling everything."[46] From then on, Doyle has told her readers just what feeling everything feels like. "Sadness, loss, fear, anger, anxiety—all of these things that you have been numbing with booze—you feel them for the first time."[47] It's "horrific," but it's the only way to show up authentically in the world, according to Doyle. It took her years to stop casting her anxiety as an imperfection. In her latest best-seller, *Untamed*, Doyle writes:

> Since I got sober, I have never been fine again, not for a single moment. I have been exhausted and terrified and angry. I have been overwhelmed and underwhelmed and debilitatingly depressed and anxious. I have been amazed and awed and delighted and overjoyed to bursting. I have been reminded, constantly, by the Ache: This will pass; stay close. I have been alive.[48]

Since Doyle got sober, she has never been "fine." Likewise, Kierkegaard's anxiety never went away. He remained "enveloped" by that "mute disquietude of thought" for the rest of his short life.[49] Even three years before he died, he was still "stifled" by it.[50] But he believed that there are better and worse ways to be anxious. We might not think of Kierkegaard as a model for how to be anxious, but we don't have to see him that way in order to listen to him.

Toward the end of Kierkegaard's life, he wrote, "Whoever has learned to be anxious in the right way has learned the ultimate."[51] Society has given us a wrong way to be anxious. It has told us that anxiety is an obstacle to living "normally." It suggests that we find coping mechanisms to quiet those terrible voices. It has equipped us poorly for the storm.

Even if Kierkegaard never learned to be anxious in the right way, Glennon Doyle has. Since she got sober, she has come up with a better way to deal with anxiety. She created a nonprofit organization that shares money and resources with people who need it. Now anxious in the right way, she hears fire alarms all over the world and she finds fires that need putting out. Doyle's story is Kierkegaardian: Anxious people are not broken. We are anxious *and* whole. Adopting this idea is one way to begin being anxious "in the right way." And by "grasping our human condition—our finiteness, our brief time in the light," Yalom adds, we can "increase our compassion for ourselves and for all other human beings."[52]

Even in the severest cases, anxious people are not broken.[53] The world is toxic, and every day we ingest its toxins in seemingly harmless messaging like "Amazing Things Happen When You Try." Ask the people who try on a daily basis. See if amazing things are happening for them, or if they find themselves stuck in the same shame-riddled world where bad things eventually happen. Do not ask the self-help authors who manifested their dreams and charge you money to tell you that you're doing it wrong.

All of this Kierkegaardian advice does not adequately address the fact that, although anxiety is unpleasant for most of us, it's debilitating for a small percentage of us. It hurts to dwell on our eternal emptiness, perpetual mutability, or the final fact of our death. It can be torturous to live in your own head hearing nothing but the voice of doom. If medication can lower the volume on the voice, take it, but never forget that you and your loved ones are condemned to death, sooner or later. We can choose to turn either against our anxiety or toward it—to disable a fire alarm to avoid the inconvenience of malfunction or to keep it in working order. As with depression, Plato *and* Prozac can help us deal with anxiety.

Kierkegaard's experience with anxiety helped him see in the dark. He felt his way around his cave long enough to conclude that anxiety is a sign of intelligence. Kierkegaard's story paints anxiety as constantly forcing us to look down into the abyss. It's a *daimon* who reminds us that we're alone and mortal. It's a fire alarm that can be both unbearable and thrilling. It's a critique of the #StayPositive messaging that cannot stand to admit that children die. As brutal as it can be, anxiety makes us 100 percent human: gritty and scared, bloody and present. This portrait may not make anxiety look super-attractive, but it keeps us on our own side.

After initial resistance to the idea that her anxiety might not be all bad, Eva reported feeling validated by Kierkegaard's philosophy. "I don't like my anxiety any better," she said, "but I feel more normal now. And smarter." Eva was someone who had never talked openly about anxiety before the class, and Kierkegaard taught her how to be anxious and dignified. She walked into the classroom believing that anxiety made her broken. She walked out feeling whole and excruciatingly alive to the world.

conclusion

practicing night vision

In college, I thought the prisoners in Plato's cave were ignorant because they weren't enlightened. I had failed to consider the puppeteers.

Anyone who casts shadows and then asks us to believe what we see is a puppeteer. One exceptionally interesting detail that Plato leaves out is whether the puppeteers know what they are doing. "Are they prisoners too?" my students ask. "Are they fooling people on purpose?" I don't know, I tell the students. Maybe some are and some aren't. Maybe they're all prisoners.

In this book, a puppeteer is anyone selling us light or asking us to see darkness as ugly, ill, ignorant, or broken. Maybe we are the puppeteer. Maybe we have said to a disappointed kid: "You get what you get and you don't get upset."* Maybe we have told loved ones to lighten up. Maybe we have told ourselves to. Regardless, we should be vigilant about noticing the anti-darkness messages we surround ourselves with and propagate.

We can take from Plato's cave a warning: everyone is a potential puppeteer. All storytellers—writers, actors, therapists,

---

* Even in cases where it's true that we can't change what life hands us, why the prohibition against getting upset about it?

scientists, social media influencers, news anchors, doctors, clergy, politicians—have the power to throw shadows. They all ask us to believe the words they tell us rather than helping us find our own words. Every semester I tell my students not to believe me. I have them buy the original texts of the philosophers we study so they can interpret for themselves what the philosophers say and not take my word for it. I remind them that I am a storyteller and there are many ways to tell a story.

In a popular Native American parable typically attributed to the Cherokee or Lenape people, a wise man tells his grandson that there are two wolves fighting inside of him: a good one and a bad one, a peaceful one and an angry one, a light one and a dark one. The scared grandson asks: "Which wolf will win?" "It depends on which one you feed," replies the sage. The Light Metaphor would have us interpret this story as meaning that we ought not to give in to moods like grief and anger, which some Buddhists refer to as "destructive emotions." Too often we have heard it said that negativity makes us sick, and that if we stop indulging our dark moods they will die down. The light wolf will win. We will become all light.

But deep inside we know that becoming all light is not an option.

Socrates once told a story about learning. He said that every time we think we're learning—gaining new information—we're actually summoning wisdom from our deepest selves. He called it *recollection*, the idea that we already know things but need help bringing them to the surface. The fact that we will never be all light, no matter how long we starve ourselves, is like that. It's not new. But we forget it over and over again and need help recollecting it. Even my kid's soccer coach, who wears a #NOBADDAYS T-shirt, must know, at some deep level, that it makes no sense. There's no such thing as all good days. There is no one on the planet whose light wolf destroyed their dark wolf. There are no all-light wolves, or all-light humans. What my kid's soccer coach forgets each morning as he goes hunting in his drawer is that his shirt—like the positivity posters at the airport (IT WILL GET BRIGHTER!), like the self-help books that tell us *Happiness Is a Choice*—sets a standard we can only fall short of, since even one bad day means we've failed.

But we have bad days. And we have plenty of good reasons to feel bad, to grieve, to be sad, anxious, angry, depressed. Meanwhile, joy is elusive, but it probably comes from a feeling of being accepted *as we are* more than from motivational posters telling us to try harder. The Light Metaphor relentlessly suggests we fly higher, be brighter, but like Icarus, we have wings made of wax. They melt when we get too close to the sun, and we fall back to the cool Earth, where trees can provide us with much needed shade. And just as Icarus's wings were not a flaw in his design, dark moods are not flaws in ours. Anxiety, depression, and the other dark moods explored in this book do not make us weak or broken. They do make us vulnerable to over-exposure, reminding us that humans are not fit for so much sunshine. We need a shady tree to rest under, and a nice long sleep every night.

Not feeding the dark wolf inside of us, far from killing it, will only make it extremely cranky. We have tried starving out the dark wolf on a diet of positive affirmations, only to grow ashamed when it refuses to die. If we want our two fighting wolves to get along, we'd be well advised not to starve either one.

What if we tried feeding the dark wolf? What if we gave it what it needs, like love and understanding, empathy and company? Maybe then it would settle down on a rug next to the fire. By feeding it well, we might begin to see its new coat grow in, thick and shiny. Eventually it might even seek out the light wolf, not to dominate it but to play. Maybe at night the two wolves, light and dark, will curl up together at our feet.

To see in the dark, we need to learn to sit still in the cave. We also need some *dolores* to test out our new approach, but we don't need to go looking for them. Life hands them to us for free, like the guy on Canal Street who thrusts a flyer for a Statue of Liberty boat tour into our hands. Likewise, we don't have to call our painful moods "gifts," and we don't have to be grateful for them. We need only think and speak about our moods in ways that don't forfeit our dignity. It would help if our society could dim the lights a bit and take down some posters long enough to help us stop turning against ourselves.

As our spelunking guides, the philosophers in this book have offered us stories that emphasize the dignity of darkness instead of its dysfunction. They have left us evidence that dark moods can give us access to connection, compassion, love, creativity, justice, motivation, and self-knowledge. Remembering the wisdom of these philosophers can help us stay on our own side, instead of turning against ourselves, when things get difficult.

We can try respecting our anxiety, as Kierkegaard did his own, instead of calling it names. Kierkegaard reminds us that anxiety makes us humans and not tables, so taking an adversarial stance against it amounts to denying our humanity. In the very old story he tells, anxiety is the uniquely human concern about life and death. It's the voice reminding us that we are fragile beings who will surely die, and that we need to do something about it even as the rest of the world snoozes. The way anxiety tunes in to the world's chaos and possibilities can feel extremely disconcerting, but it's not wrong. Life is chaotic, we are mortal, and everything good we have can disappear. Anxiety is a sign of emotional intelligence.

A better story about anxiety will not kill the dark wolf, but that's not the goal. Some degree of anxiety is necessary if we are to live as though we are dying, love deeply and fiercely, and deal honestly with pain and loss. Learning to be anxious in the right way might entail finding a good therapist and taking medication until the voices speak to us at a reasonable volume. Then we can listen to our anxiety and use it to connect with loved ones before they're on their deathbeds.

Like Anzaldúa, we can invent new metaphors for old moods. She didn't befriend her depression, but she renamed it. With a new vocabulary based on Aztec mythology, Anzaldúa gave depression a job in her knowledge production. Coatlicue confronted Anzaldúa with her "lazy" narrative, forcing her to recognize that it was a by-product of sexism, racism, and homophobia. Anzaldúa's worry about being a popcorn theorist ran deep, but sitting in the dark showed her she wasn't the only Woman of Color made to feel like a phony by a society that thinks it knows what a theorist (or doctor, janitor, nurse, lawyer, or flight attendant) looks like. Anzaldúa's myth did not kill her depression, but it did give her a way out of the Brokenness Story. It also provided her with the means to point to society's brokenness. A new vocabulary can win us self-respect, and it can also help us identify the external sources of our anguish.

We might choose to refuse phony condolences and to live in the truth of our misery, as C. S. Lewis did. He knew his grief made him irascible to friends and family, but he stayed on his own side. We have no need to hide our grief just because it makes other people squirm. They will squirm when they see it for the first time, but people who truly love and respect us will make room for our dark wolf to come get some attention. And when the wolf of grief wants to rest, to sit at our feet instead of in our lap, loved ones will no longer call that "getting over it."

We can teach them that grief is something we carry forever. After all, most people have only ever learned to run away when they pass a cave of grief, not how to enter it, sit in the dark, and hold space for *dolor*.

Granted their dignity, our dark moods remind us that congenital analgesia (the inability to feel pain) is not something to aspire to. Unamuno's life was full of suffering, but he learned not to mistake suffering for a character flaw or illness. He stayed on his own side instead of turning on himself. If we too could remind ourselves every time we feel pain that our pain is not a sign of being "too sensitive," if we could imagine *dolor* as bestowing upon us a sixth sense, then we might be more tempted to look around, head high, until we spot a fellow sufferer. If misery loves company, let's use it to find one another.

Finally, learning to see in the dark enables us to reenvision anger. Lugones left us with the pearl of wisdom that there is not one anger but many. Together, our angers form what Lorde called an "arsenal"—the store of weapons we need to fight injustice.[1] Instead of counting to ten or smothering our angers, we can be like bell hooks and criticize the framing of anger by professionals in various fields as irrational, crazy, or ugly. Despite Lugones's ambivalence about her own anger, she left us with a new way to talk about anger that can help us distinguish between ugly anger and anger that is not ugly, between first- and second-order anger. She left behind meaningful insights that can help angry people feel dignified. Finally, if we remember that angers are meant to be used, not diffused, we can learn to train them instead of trying to control them. Seeing in the dark can teach us how best to use our angers in our personal and political lives.

In practicing night vision, it's important to keep in mind that the new stories we tell about our dark moods need not simply oppose or replace the medical stories we have learned about disease, diagnosis, and treatment. Medical understandings of mental health are not going away, nor should they. They enable us to get the medical care that can help us see in the dark (and fit in to a nyctophobic society). But alongside these medicalized narratives, we can tell a parallel story to ourselves and each other, a philosophical one that returns dignity to the moods that our society shames.

A hundred years from now, maybe society will have gotten over its fear of emotional darkness. By then maybe we will have realized that expecting people to be perpetually cheerful leaves them unable to deal with difficult moods. Maybe we will have smashed all the coffee mugs instructing us to MAKE TODAY RIDICULOUSLY AMAZING. Henry David Thoreau once poetically referred, with great admiration, to "the night in which the corn grows."[2] We too can recollect that night is not just scary and dangerous, but also fertile, germinal, alive.

In an emotionally intelligent future, no one will conflate grief lasting more than two weeks with a mental disorder. People will speak about depression as more than a mental health issue. We will answer honestly when someone asks how we are, since we will no longer be expected to hide or belittle our dark moods, to "put on a brave face." No one will call "First World Problems" on us or tell us that someone at Auschwitz would kill to trade places with us (as a well-intentioned friend once said to me when I was feeling down). There are lots of boneheaded things—all variations on "look on the bright side"—that people will no longer say in a more emotionally intelligent future. As we set to work building *el mundo zurdo*, we can help everyone gain night vision.

At the end of the semester, I tell my students not to be surprised if they learn the wrong lesson. The moment you think you're learning something, I tell them, is the time to be the most careful, the most discerning. It's the moment when you have to ask yourself if you're not just swapping one shadow for another.

In college, Plato taught me the importance of doubt. But as my students do every semester, I doubted the wrong thing. In doubting trees but not light, I had only swapped one shadow for another. It took me years to realize that light cannot save us from darkness, and it took me even longer to see that darkness is not what imprisons us.

I hope this book helps you personally. But that's not all I want.

My wish is that you will catch yourself the next time you are about to invoke the Light Metaphor—that you will pause when you're about to share your "lightbulb moment" or explain how a book "shed light on" a problem that's puzzled you for years; that you will never again claim to see the light at the end of the tunnel without considering that you might be leaving someone stuck in there; that you will stop comparing anything to night and day; that you will not think of difficulties as problems in need of illumination; that you will refrain from telling anyone, especially yourself, to look on the bright side. It is also my hope that you will think about the ramifications of starting any sentence with "At least. . . ." Instead, I urge you to recollect and keep close the idea that darkness is a reality to acclimate to, to feel your way around in, and to see yourself and others in. Doubt the shadow that casts darkness as deficiency. You can get what you get and still be upset. Allowing yourself to be upset might even help you realize what you truly want.

Somewhere along the way to developing night vision you will need to become convinced that emotional pain can be used as a conduit to community, connection, self-knowledge, accuracy, wisdom, empathy, and intelligence. You'll also need to believe that we who live with these moods never lose our dignity, even when we are splayed out on the bathroom floor.

But don't take my word for it. Don't accept my conclusion about the wicked sprawl of the Light Metaphor and its doppelgänger, the Brokenness Story. I'm going for recollection here. Does the image I have given you—of an emotional world that binges on light but is starved for shade—resonate in your core? If it doesn't, leave it and find a better explanation for why so many people feel ashamed of their difficult moods. If it does resonate, though, you are very likely summoning a truth that has been buried under layer upon layer of insipid inspirational aphorisms. To know whether dark moods look more natural and less scary in the dark, practice night vison and see for yourself.

acknowledgments

Thank you to the University of Texas Rio Grande Valley, which supported the writing of this book by awarding me a faculty development leave in 2020–2021. To my philosophy majors, minors, and graduates: people who look like us or speak Spanglish are not mere consumers of other people's ideas. *Somos filósofos*, creators of knowledge. When you look in the mirror, say: *This is what a philosopher looks like.*

To Markus Hoffman, thank you for trying to sell my brand of pessimism in 2014, when the United States was still delirious with hope. To Rob Tempio, your enthusiasm and kindness relaxed me into writing honestly. To the production and marketing team at Princeton University Press, especially Chloe Coy, Sara Lerner, David Campbell, Maria Whelan, and Laurie Schlesinger: thank you for *getting* it. Thanks to Cynthia Buck for eliminating my ambiguous antecedents and to Michael Flores for taking such care with the index.

Kemlo Aki, without you, no book. You helped me kick the worst of my academic writing habits. You're the best kind of tough. Jill Angel, thank you for keeping me consistent.

Reine, Brad, Marilyn, Gordon, and Amy, thank you for cheering me on at so early a stage. Katie, Yael, and Tina, you identified the places that hurt with a compassionate pen, and your comments helped me write what I meant. Thank you for not letting me go outside with no pants on. Thanks always to

John Kaag, who was convinced I had something to say before I was.

Lodly and Jenn, when we were kids, we sensed that complaining is communion and that laughing + crying = life. JTLS, for twenty years you've let me talk in extremes before reaching my conclusions. You're wicked smart.

To my ten-year-old, Santiago Emerson: you're a watcher, and you inspire me to look carefully at other people, at myself, and at our society. *Nunca dejes de abrazarme.*

To my eight-year-old, Sebastián Pascal, *mi principe, mi tesoro, mi corazón*: watching you play reminds me that I'm a body too. *Eres único en todo este mundo.*

To Alex, who put a hundred hours into consoling me and another hundred into reading drafts, chapters, sections, paragraphs, sentences, phrases, and words: your love works. *Te quiero tal y como eres.*

All the remaining blunders are for you to name, dear reader, in the service of creating a better world. I look forward to this book's obsolescence, to the time when we cry without apology. Thank you for caring.

notes

Introduction. Doubting the Light

1. The best-selling author Glennon Doyle inspired this reframe. In a Twitter post, she wrote: "Q: G, Why do you cry so often? A: For the same reason I laugh so often. Because I'm paying attention." Glennon Doyle, Twitter post, November 2015, https://twitter.com/glennondoyle/status/661634542311223296?lang=en.

2. Jean Paul Sartre, *No Exit and Three Other Plays*, translated by Stuart Gilbert (New York: Vintage, 1989), 45; and Søren Kierkegaard, *Søren Kierkegaard's Journals and Papers*, edited and translated by Howard V. Hong and Edna H. Hong (Bloomington: Indiana University Press, 1967), 6.470 entry 6837 (X.5 A 72, n.d., 1853).

3. If you're wondering why I want to call these thinkers "philosophers" even though some of them didn't even earn a PhD, here's the reason. Besides ancient Greek philosophers like Socrates, Plato, and Aristotle, who existed before PhDs did, countless men throughout history have been granted the title without earning the degree. René Descartes, the famous French philosopher who said, "I think, therefore I am," did not have a degree in philosophy. Friedrich Nietzsche, whom most people would label a philosopher even if they never read him, was not trained in philosophy, nor did he teach it. A more contemporary example is the British theorist Derek Parfit, who is listed as a philosopher on Wikipedia despite not having earned a PhD in philosophy. Contrast these examples to the Black intellectual bell hooks, whom Wikipedia labels as an "American author, professor, feminist, and social activist," or the Black poet Audre Lorde, an "American writer, feminist, womanist, librarian, and civil rights activist." Their philosophies of anger explored in the next chapter can shift our thinking, but academic philosophy still mostly keeps them out of the classroom. Throughout history, the back door to professional philosophy has opened readily for white men but not so easily for Women of Color.

4. Wendell Berry, "To Know the Dark," in *New Collected Poems* (Berkeley, CA: Counterpoint Press, 2012). Copyright © 1970, 2012 by Wendell Berry. Reprinted with the permission of The Permissions Company, LLC on behalf of Counterpoint Press, counterpointpress.com.

Chapter 1. Getting Honest about Anger

1. Only 20 percent of philosophy faculty are women, and only 3 percent are non-white. Out of the 6,700 full- and part-time faculty members counted in 2017, roughly 1,400 were women. Only 200 were nonwhite men and women. Justin Weinberg, "Facts and Figures about US Philosophy Departments," *Daily Nous*, May 18, 2020, https://dailynous.com/2020/05/18/facts-figures-philosophy-departments-united-states/.

2. Carlos Alberto Sánchez, "Philosophy and the Post-Immigrant Fear," *Philosophy in the Contemporary World* 18, no. 1 (2011): 39.

3. Kristie Dotson, "How Is This Paper Philosophy?," *Comparative Philosophy* 3, no. 1 (2012): 3–29. For more on the exclusion of Women of Color from academia see Joy James, "Teaching Theory, Talking Community" in *Spirit, Space, and Survival: African American Women in (White) Academe* (New York: Routledge, 1993), 118–38.

4. Plato, *Phaedrus*, translated by Alexander Nehemas and Paul Woodruff (Indianapolis: Hackett, 1995), 253e.

5. Michael Potegal and Raymond W. Novaco, "A Brief History of Anger," in *International Handbook of Anger: Constituent and Concomitant Biological, Psychological, and Social Processes*, edited by Michael Potegal, Gerhard Stemmler, and Charles Spielberger (New York: Springer, 2010), 9–24.

6. Seneca, *De Ira*, book III, section 12.

7. Epictetus, *The Handbook* (*The Enchiridion*), translated by Nicholas White (Indianapolis: Hackett Publishing Co., 1983), 13.

8. Potegal and Novaco, "A Brief History of Anger," 16.

9. Marcus Aurelius, *Meditations*, translated by Gregory Hays (New York: Modern Library, 2003), 38.

10. Ibid., 17.

11. Pierre Hadot, *Philosophy as a Way of Life: Spiritual Exercises from Socrates to Foucault*, translated by Michael Chase (Malden: Blackwell, 1995), chap. 9.

12. "Imaginary Friends," episode 1,647 of *Mister Rogers' Neighborhood*, directed by Bob Walsh, aired on PBS (WQED), February 25, 1992.

13. Potegal and Novaco, "A Brief History of Anger," 15.

14. Ibid., 15–16.

15. Ibid.

16. Mark Manson, *The Subtle Art of Not Giving a F*ck: A Counterintuitive Approach to Living a Good Life* (New York: HarperCollins, 2016).

17. Mark Manson, "Why I Am Not a Stoic," Mark Manson: Life Advice That Doesn't Suck (blog), n.d., https://markmanson.net/why-i-am-not-a-stoic.

18. Gary John Bishop, *Stop Doing That Sh*t: End Self-Sabotage and Demand Your Life Back* (San Francisco: HarperOne, 2019).

19. Her biographer Alexis De Veaux calls Audre Lorde a "living philosopher," borrowing the concept from Joy James. See Alexis De Veaux, *Warrior Poet: A Biography of Audre Lorde* (New York: W. W. Norton and Co., 2004), 35; and Joy James, "African Philosophy, Theory, and 'Living Thinkers,'" in *Spirit, Space, and Survival: African American Women in (White) Academe*, edited by Joy James and Ruth Farmer (New York: Routledge, 1993), 31–46.

20. Audre Lorde, "The Uses of Anger: Women Responding to Racism," in Audre Lorde, *Sister Outsider: Essays and Speeches* (New York: Random House/Crossing Press, 2007), 124.

21. Ibid., 127.

22. Ibid., 129.

23. Ibid.

24. Myisha Cherry, *The Case for Rage: Why Anger Is Essential to Anti-Racist Struggle* (Oxford: Oxford University Press, 2021).

25. Lorde, "The Uses of Anger," 127.

26. Ibid., 125.

27. Ibid.

28. Ibid., 130.

29. Soraya Chemaly, *Rage Becomes Her: The Power of Women's Anger* (New York: Atria Books, 2018), 51.

30. Ibid., 51–52.

31. Ibid., 54.

32. Lorde, "The Uses of Anger," 128.

33. Joseph P. Williams, "The US Capitol Riots and the Double Standard of Protest Policing," *U.S. News & World Report*, January 12, 2021, https://www.usnews.com/news/national-news/articles/2021-01-12/the-us-capitol-riots-and-the-double-standard-of-protest-policing.

34. Jolie McCullough, "'We Would Have Been Shot': Texas Activists Shaken by Law Enforcement Reaction to Capitol Siege," *Texas Tribune*, January 7, 2021, www.texastribune.org/2021/01/07/capitol-siege-police-response-difference/.

35. Madelyn Beck, "A BLM Protest Brought Thousands of National Guardsmen to DC in June. Where Were They Wednesday?," *Boise State Public Radio News*, January 8, 2021, https://www.boisestatepublicradio.org/post/blm-protest-brought-thousands-national-guardsmen-dc-june-where-were-they-wednesday#stream/0.

36. NPR's Steve Inkseep King interviewed the chair of Princeton University's Department of African American Studies, Eddie Glaude, about the differing responses to the Capitol incident and the BLM protests. See Steve Inkseep King, "Comparing Police Responses To Pro-Trump Mob, Racial Justice Protests," NPR, January 7, 2021, https://www.npr.org/2021/01/07/954324564/comparing-police-responses-to-pro-trump

-mob-racial-justice-protests; see also Nicole Chavez, "Rioters Breached US Capitol Security on Wednesday. This Was the Police Response When It Was Black Protesters on DC Streets Last Year," CNN, January 10, 2021, https://www.cnn.com/2021/01/07 /us/police-response-black-lives-matter-protest-us-capitol/index.html.

37. Thousands of people, from the civil rights movement until today, have been arrested for sitting down where they ought not to, and yet none of the men with guns and knives who broke glass and crushed bodies were arrested while doing so. By not protecting the Capitol with riot police or letting the National Guard members carry weapons, the DC government was publicly giving the benefit of the doubt to rioters after having failed to give it to Black Lives Matter protesters. Ten thousand nonviolent BLM protesters all over the country were arrested, including 316 in DC in one night. See Michael Sainato, "'They Set Us Up': US Police Arrested over 10,000 Protesters, Many Non-violent," *Guardian*, June 8, 2020, https://www.theguardian.com/us-news /2020/jun/08/george-floyd-killing-police-arrest-non-violent-protesters; see also Eliott C. McLaughlin, "On These 9 Days, Police in DC Arrested More People than They Did during the Capitol Siege," CNN, January 12, 2021, https://www.cnn.com/2021/01 /11/us/dc-police-previous-protests-capitol/index.html. McLaughlin writes, "On two separate days in July, Capitol Police confirmed to CNN officers had arrested 80 and then 155 protesters who had entered the halls of Congress to engage in peaceful protests—sit-ins, chanting, lying on the ground and the like." See also Vince Dixon, "How Arrests in the Capitol Riot Compare to That of Black Lives Matter Protests," *Boston Globe*, January 7, 2021, https://www.bostonglobe.com/2021/01/07/nation /how-arrests-capitol-riot-wednesday-compare-that-black-lives-matter-protests/.

38. Jay Reeves, Lisa Mascaro, and Calvin Woodward, "Capitol Assault a More Sinister Attack than First Appeared," Associated Press, January 11, 2021, https:// apnews.com/article/us-capitol-attack-14c73ee280c256ab4ec193ac0f49ad54.

39. Ibid.; see also Julie Gerstein, "Officers Calmly Posed for Selfies and Appeared to Open Gates for Protesters during the Madness of the Capitol Building Insurrection," *Business Insider*, January 7, 2021, https://www.businessinsider.com/capitol -building-officers-posed-for-selfies-helped-protesters-2021-1.

40. It took an excessively long time for people whose job it was to shut riots down to perceive this group of angry white men as violent and dangerous. See Lauren Giella, "Fact Check: Did Trump Call in the National Guard after Rioters Stormed the Capitol?" *Newsweek*, January 8, 2021, https://www.newsweek.com/fact-check-did -trump-call-national-guard-after-rioters-stormed-capitol-1560186.

41. Abby Llorico, "2 St. Louis Area Men Charged in Connection with Capitol Riots," Fox43, February 5, 2021, https://www.fox43.com/article/news/crime/two-st -louis-area-men-charged-capitol-riots/63-06b8a7c5-bd64-40a4-8ead-b81293bf 4484.

42. bell hooks, *Killing Rage: Ending Racism* (New York: Henry Holt and Co., 1995), 12.

43. Ibid.

44. Ibid.

45. María Lugones, *Pilgrimages/Peregrinajes: Theorizing Coalition against Multiple Oppressions* (Lanham, MD: Rowman and Littlefield, 2003), chap. 5.

46. Lugones, *Pilgrimages/Peregrinajes*, 19.

47. Carleton Office of the Chaplain, "Farewells: Maria Lugones," July 16, 2020, https://www.carleton.edu/farewells/maria-lugones/; see also Jennifer Micale, "Thought and Practice: María Lugones Leaves a Global Legacy," *BingUNews*, August 7, 2020, https://www.binghamton.edu/news/story/2580/thought-and-practice-maria-lugones-leaves-a-global-legacy.

48. Lugones, *Pilgrimages/Peregrinajes*, 106.

49. Ibid.

50. Ibid., 18.

51. Potegal and Novaco, "A Brief History of Anger," 13–14.

52. Ibid., 14.

53. Lugones, *Pilgrimages/Peregrinajes*, 107.

54. Ibid.

55. Ibid., 117.

56. Ibid.

57. Ibid., 105.

58. Ibid., 111.

59. Myisha Cherry observes that many so-called anger-management techniques haven't really been employed in the service of being a good manager of anger so much as "simply firing unruly employees." Cherry, *The Case for Rage*, 139.

60. Chemaly, *Rage Becomes Her*, 260.

61. Miranda Fricker, *Epistemic Injustice: Power and the Ethics of Knowing* (Oxford: Oxford University Press, 2007).

62. Lugones, *Pilgrimages/Peregrinajes*, 105.

63. Lama Rod Owens, *Love and Rage: The Path of Liberation through Anger* (Berkeley, CA: North Atlantic Books, 2020).

64. Howard Thurman, *Jesus and the Disinherited* (Nashville: Abingdon-Cokesbury Press, 1949).

Chapter 2. I Suffer, Therefore I Am

1. See Jerome Wakefield and Allan V. Horwitz, *The Loss of Sadness: How Psychiatry Transformed Normal Sorrow into Depressive Disorder* (Oxford: Oxford University Press, 2007).

2. Epicurus calls it a "tempest of the soul." See "Letter to Menoeceus," in Diogenes Laertius, *Lives of Eminent Philosophers*, vol. II, translated by R. D. Hicks (Cambridge, MA: Harvard University Press, 1995), 655.

3. In his "Letter to Menoeceus," Epicurus suggests a "four-part cure" to remedy the storm in the soul: "Don't fear god, don't worry about death; what's good is easy to get, and what's terrible is easy to endure." He also tried to help us by distinguishing between types of desires—natural versus unnatural and necessary versus unnecessary—and claimed that our best desires are those that are both natural and necessary. The most dangerous desires for us are unnatural and unnecessary, since they will be hardest to attain and are likely to bring us misery. If we could only figure out which desires are which and only desire those we can acquire easily, we could be happier.

4. Epicurus, "Letter to Menoeceus."

5. Diane Alber, *A Little Spot of Sadness: A Story about Empathy and Compassion* (Gilbert, AZ: Diane Alber Art LLC, 2019).

6. For Jody's story, see Martin Seligman, Karen Reivich, Lisa Jaycox, and Jane Gillham, *The Optimistic Child: A Proven Program to Safeguard Children against Depression and Build Lifelong Resilience* (Boston: Houghton Mifflin, 1995), 100–102.

7. Ibid., 100.

8. Ibid., 101 (emphasis in original).

9. Ibid.

10. Ibid. (emphasis in original).

11. Ibid., 102.

12. Ibid., 144.

13. In *The Tragic Sense of Life*, Unamuno asks why Descartes did not use the formal "*Siento, luego soy*" (I feel, therefore I am). Since the book turns on suffering, I take Unamuno's question as referring not to feeling in general but to feeling *dolor* in particular. Miguel de Unamuno, *Del sentimiento tragico de la vida en los hombres y en los pueblos y Tratado del amor de dios*, edited by Nelson Orringer (Madrid: Editorial Tecnos, 2005), 141; see also *The Tragic Sense of Life in Men and Nations*, translated by Anthony Kerrigan (Princeton, NJ: Princeton University Press, 1972), 41.

14. Three months before the start of the Spanish-American War, the thirty-four-year-old Unamuno told a friend, "*Mi vida es un constante meditation mortis*" (my life is a constant meditation on death). See Hernán Benítez, *El drama religioso de Unamuno* (Buenos Aires: Universidad de Buenos Aires, Instituto de Publicaciones, 1949), 255–63.

15. The original Spanish reads: "Y lo mas de mi labor ha sido siempre inquietar a mis prójimos, removerles el poso del corazón, angustiarlos si puedo." Miguel de Unamuno, *Mi religion y otros ensayos breves* (Buenos Aires: Espasa Calpe, 1942), 13. The

translation is from Miguel de Unamuno, "My Religion," in *Selected Works of Miguel de Unamuno*, vol. 5, *The Agony of Christianity and Essays on Faith*, translated by Anthony Kerrigan (Princeton, NJ: Princeton University Press, 1974), 214. For variations in translation, see also Miguel de Unamuno, "My Religion," in *Essays and Soliloquies*, translated by J. E. Crawford Flitch (New York: Alfred A. Knopf, 1925), 159; Miguel de Unamuno, *Perplexities and Paradoxes*, translated by Stuart Gross (New York: Philosophical Library, 1945), 5; and Miguel de Unamuno, "My Religion," translated by Armaund Baker, https://www.armandfbaker.com/translations/unamuno/my _religion.pdf.

16. Miguel de Unamuno, *Our Lord Don Quixote: The Life of Don Quixote and Sancho, with Related Essays* (Princeton, NJ: Princeton University Press, 1967), 305.

17. Lorde, "The Uses of Anger," 127.

18. Unamuno, *The Tragic Sense of Life*, 149.

19. Unamuno, "My Religion" (*Perplexities and Paradoxes*), 6.

20. This phrase is used by the psychologist Barbara Held to denote the cultural messages we receive to "look on the bright side" of negative situations. Held, "The Tyranny of the Positive Attitude in America: Observation and Speculation," *Journal of Clinical Psychology* 58, no. 9 (September 2002): 965–91.

21. Lore has it that Unamuno called himself the "high priest" of the "temple of intelligence," and that while the Francoists might very well conquer (*vencer*), they would never convince (*convencer*). Although he probably did not speak these exact words, whatever Unamuno said must have been fierce, because he was promptly removed from his rectorship a second time. Severiano Delgado's compelling historical research suggests that Luis Portillo put those poetic words in Unamuno's mouth for his article "Unamuno's Last Lecture," published in *Horizon* in 1941. See Sam Jones, "Spanish Civil War Speech Invented by Father of Michael Portillo, Says Historian," *Guardian*, May 11, 2018, https://www.theguardian.com/world/2018/may/11/famous -spanish-civil-war-speech-may-be-invented-says-historian.

22. A bilingual student of mine once objected to the translation of Unamuno's term *compasión* as "pity" in the most affordable English edition of the text. She argued that pity is not compassion, and that Unamuno could not really have believed that "everyone wants to be pitied." This student supposed that few people really want pity, but that a great many want compassion, sympathy, or empathy. Since these terms slosh and slide into one another linguistically, we can adopt some stipulative distinctions. If pity says, "I feel sorry for you," and empathy says, "I feel your pain," compassion dares to say, "I feel you feeling your pain and feel it with you." If we agree with my student that Unamuno probably did not mean that people want to be pitied, then we can settle on compassion as a good goal. Unamuno believed that we want to be grasped in our sorrow, physically and/or emotionally. Like Jody, we want to be

reached for. Compassion does that. It moves toward instead of away from a suffering individual. Unamuno, *The Tragic Sense of Life*, 153.

23. Ibid., 150.

24. Ibid., 147–49.

25. *My Dinner with Andre* was a 1981 film in which André Gregory and Wallace Shawn have an existential conversation about suffering, fear, the meaning of life, happiness, and so on. In one scene, Gregory recounts the experience of being told he looked "wonderful!" by seven or eight people. Only one woman told him he looked "horrible." He began to tell her some of the troubles he was having, at which point she burst into tears and told him about her aunt being in the hospital. This woman was the only person who really saw him, he said, though "she didn't know anything about what I've been going through." He thought that, "because this had happened to her very very recently, she could see me with complete clarity. The other people, what they saw, was this tan, or this shirt, or the fact that the shirt goes well with the tan." Gregory was making Unamuno's point about suffering people being able to see other suffering people. See Wallace Shawn and André Gregory, *My Dinner with Andre: A Screenplay for the Film by Louis Malle* (New York: Grove Press, 1994), 60–61, https://fliphtml5.com/dyfu/uedt/basic; for this scene in the film, see "*My Dinner with Andre* (1981)," minute 50:55, https://www.youtube.com/watch?v=O4lvOjiHFw0.

26. Unamuno, "My Religion" (*Perplexities and Paradoxes*), 6.

27. Ibid.

Chapter 3. Grieving Stubbornly

1. Leeat Granek, "Grief as Pathology: The Evolution of Grief Theory in Psychology from Freud to the Present," *History of Psychology* 13, no. 1 (2010): 48.

2. Katherine May, *Wintering: The Power of Rest and Retreat in Difficult Times* (London: Ebury Publishing, 2020).

3. Seneca, "Consolation to Marcia," in *Dialogues and Essays*, translated by John Davie (Oxford: Oxford University Press, 2008), 55–56.

4. Ibid., 54.

5. Ibid., 60.

6. Ibid., 57.

7. Ibid., 63.

8. Seneca wrote: "I am unable to tackle such hardened sorrow in a kind or gentle manner." Ibid., 55. See also "Consolation to Helvia," in *Dialogues and Essays*, 165.

9. Ibid., 164.

10. Seneca, "Consolation to Marcia," 70.

11. Seneca, "Consolaton to Helvia," 161.

12. Seneca, "Consolation to Marcia," 57.

13. Cicero, *Cicero on the Emotions: Tusculan Disputations 3 and 4*, edited and translated by Margaret Graver (Chicago: University of Chicago Press, 2002), 28, 111, 114.

14. Ibid., 31.

15. Epictetus, *The Handbook*, 12.

16. Ibid., 12.

17. Origen, *Contra Celcus*, book VII, Early Christian Writings, http://www.earlychristianwritings.com/text/origen167.html.

18. Seneca, *Letters from a Stoic* (London: Penguin Books, 2004), 87, 212.

19. Montaigne was forty-seven when his essays were published. See Montaigne, "On Affectionate Relationships," in *The Complete Essays* (London: Penguin Books, 1993), 205–19.

20. For an account of the final days of La Boétie's life, see Sarah Blakewell, *How to Live, or A Life of Montaigne in One Question and Twenty Attempts at an Answer* (London: Chatto & Windus, 2010), 90–108.

21. Montaigne, "On Affectionate Relationships," 212.

22. Ibid., 217.

23. Ibid., 218.

24. Ibid.

25. To learn how chimpanzees carry around their dead, see Marc Bekoff, *The Emotional Lives of Animals: A Leading Scientist Explores Animal Joy, Sorrow, and Empathy—and Why They Matter* (Novato, CA: New World Library, 2008).

26. American Psychiatric Association, *Diagnostic and Statistical Manual of Mental Disorders*, 5th ed. (*DSM-5*) (Arlington, VA: American Psychiatric Association, 2013), sect. III.

27. The *DSM-5* says: "These proposed criteria sets are not intended for clinical use; only the criteria sets and disorders in Section II of DSM-5 are officially recognized and can be used for clinical purposes." Ibid.

28. See American Psychiatric Association, "What Is Mental Illness?," https://www.psychiatry.org/patients-families/what-is-mental-illness.

29. See ClinicalTrials.gov, "A Study of Medication with or without Psychotherapy for Complicated Grief (HEAL)," US National Library of Medicine, https://www.clinicaltrials.gov/ct2/show/NCT01179568.

30. Massimo Pigliucci, "Cicero's *Tusculan Disputations: III. On Grief of Mind*," How to Be a Stoic, April 27, 2017, https://howtobeastoic.wordpress.com/2017/04/27/ciceros-tusculan-disputations-iii-on-grief-of-mind/.

31. *Cicero on the Emotions: Tusculan Disputations 3 and 4*, edited and translated by Margaret Graver (Chicago: University of Chicago Press, 2002), 11.

32. Ibid., 12.

33. Cicero continued: "Distress, of all the emotions, the one most similar to bodily illness. Desire does not resemble an infirmity, and neither does unrestrained gladness, which is excessive and wild delight of the mind. Even fear is not particularly similar to a sickness, although it is closely related to distress. But *aegritudo* specifically suggests mental pain, just as *aegrotatio*, 'infirmity,' suggests bodily pain." Ibid., 13.

34. Ibid., 14.

35. Kathleen Evans, "'Interrupted by Fits of Weeping': Cicero's Major Depressive Disorder and the Death of Tullia," in *History of Psychiatry* 18, no. 1 (2007): 86.

36. Cicero identified as a Stoic, but Stoicism seems to have been of limited use to him during his exile; indeed, his extraordinary misery and dejection was judged to be all the more remarkable in a man who described himself as a philosopher. See *Plutarch's Lives* VII: Cicero, 32. After Tullia's death, fellow Stoics like Brutus castigated Cicero for his immoderate, unseemly, and un-Stoical grief. Nonetheless, Cicero practiced Stoicism well enough to research and write "furiously" on philosophical topics to distract his attention from his suffering." See Evans, "Interrupted by Fits of Weeping," 95.

37. Evans, "Interrupted by Fits of Weeping," 86.

38. Cicero, *Tusculan Disputations* (Graver), 8.

39. This is shockingly similar to how Andrew Solomon talks about his depression, which had grown on him like a "vine" on an old oak tree, "a sucking thing that had wrapped itself around me, ugly and more alive than I. It had a life of its own that bit by bit asphyxiated all of my life out of me." See Andrew Solomon, *The Noonday Demon: An Atlas of Depression* (New York: Scribner, 2001), 18.

40. Cicero wrote: "The mind, like the body, suffers from disorders, but the medical science that might cure those disorders is littler cultivated. The source of our troubles is in false beliefs imparted to us since childhood by our families, by poetry, and by society in general: all of these teach us to value power, popularity, wealth, or pleasure above doing what is right. Such values cause people to behave badly, but also to live in emotional turmoil. The cure for this illness is to be sought in philosophy, which enable us to become our own physicians." Cicero, *Tusculan Disputations* (Graver), 73.

41. Evans, "Interrupted by Fits of Weeping." On a now deleted webpage, the World Health Organization asserted that "depression is not only the most common women's mental health problem but may be more persistent in women than men." In terms of gender bias, the WHO also previously confirmed that "doctors are more likely to diagnose depression in women compared with men, even when they have similar scores on standardized measures of depression or present with identical symptoms." The Mayo Clinic concurs that "women are nearly twice as likely as men

to be diagnosed with depression." Mayo Clinic, "Depression in Women: Understanding the Gender Gap," https://www.mayoclinic.org/diseases-conditions /depression/in-depth/depression/art-20047725.

42. Robert Burton, *The Anatomy of Melancholy*, 1621–1652, published 2009 by the Ex-Classics Project, https://www.exclassics.com/anatomy/anatint.htm.

43. Sigmund Freud, "Mourning and Melancholia," in *On the History of the Psycho-Analytic Movement*, translated by A. A. Brill (London: Hogarth Press, 1914), 243–44.

44. Leeat Granek notes that "Freud . . . in particular was clear that grief should not be considered a disorder, and that intervening with a mourner could even cause psychological damage." Granek, "Grief as Pathology," 66.

45. Ibid., 54–55; and Emil Kraepelin, *Clinical Psychiatry: A Textbook for Students and Physicians* (London: Macmillan, 1921), 115.

46. See James Gang, James Kocsis, Jonathan Avery, Paul K. Maciejewski, and Holly G. Prigerson, "Naltrexone Treatment for Prolonged Grief Disorder: Study Protocol for a Randomized, Triple-Blinded, Placebo-Controlled Trial," *Trials* 22, no. 110 (2021), https://doi.org/10.1186/s13063-021-05044-8.

47. Because of the conflation of acute grief (less than one year) with major depressive disorder, critics like Jerome Wakefield and Allan Horwitz accuse professional psychiatry of trying to pathologize a perfectly normal emotion—grief—in which a non-dysfunctional person displays depressive symptoms for more than two weeks. See Wakefield and Horwitz, *The Loss of Sadness*.

48. Sidney Zisook was aware that overdiagnosis was a risk, but he still did not want to remove the exclusion. Roger Peele was the *DSM-5* task force member who wanted everyone to stop worrying that the *DSM-5* would be implying that everyone has or will have a mental illness. He said we all suffer psychological setbacks. The midtown Manhattan study showed that 85 percent of Manhattanites suffered from life. Today it might show that 100 percent of people face setbacks and could use some therapy. But Peele also said that's very different from saying that everyone is mentally ill. Ronald Pies supported the removal of the bereavement exclusion, saying, "In my view, the term 'medicalization' has become a kind of rhetorical Rorschach test: it evokes whatever political, social, or philosophical position the reader happens to hold or wants to advocate." But even Pies rejected the two-week rule. See Sidney Zisook et al., "The Bereavement Exclusion and DSM-5," *Depression and Anxiety* 29 (2012): 425–43; Kristy Lamb, Ronald Pies, and Sidney Zisook, "The Bereavement Exclusion for the Diagnosis of Major Depression: To Be, or Not to Be," *Psychiatry* 7 no. 7 (2010); and Gary Greenberg, *Manufacturing Depression: The Secret History of a Modern Disease* (New York: Simon & Schuster, 2010), 175.

49. In 2007, Horwitz and Wakefield, criticizing the *DSM* criteria for depression in their book *The Loss of Sadness*, argued that the loss of a limb might be comparable to the

loss of a loved one. More generally, they argued that sadness is pathologized in our society; we are so uncomfortable with sadness that we overprescribe medicines designed to make us less sad. Though both authors were against removing the bereavement exclusion on the grounds that grief is not a mental illness, they also believed that other sadnesses were being medicalized and too quickly treated instead of being left alone. If anything, they might have suggested putting in more exclusions. What followed was ironic: their argument about grief was used to argue *for* removing the exclusion. The argument went like this: If loss is loss, why discriminate? See also Jerome Wakefield, Mark F. Schmitz, Michael B. First, and Allan V. Horwitz, "Extending the Bereavement Exclusion for Major Depression to Other Losses: Evidence from the National Comorbidity Survey," *Archives of General Psychiatry* 64 (April 2007): 433–40.

50. Andrew Solomon, author of *The Noonday Demon*, differentiates between major depressive disorder and grief with the longer time span of six months after a "catastrophic loss." See Andrew Solomon, "Depression, the Secret We Share," TEDxMet, October 2013, https://www.ted.com/talks/andrew_solomon_depression_the_secret_we_share/transcript?language=en.

51. See Stephen E. Gilman, Joshua Breslau, Nhi-Ha Trinh, Maurizio Fava, Jane M. Murphy, and Jordan W. Smoller, "Bereavement and the Diagnosis of Major Depressive Episode in the National Epidemiologic Survey on Alcohol and Related Conditions," *Journal of Clinical Psychiatry* 73, no. 2 (2012): 208–15.

52. C. S. Lewis, *A Grief Observed* (San Francisco: Harper & Row, 1961), 37, 39.

53. Ibid., 40.

54. Ibid., 29–30.

55. Ibid., 37.

56. Ibid., 39.

57. Ibid., 25.

58. Ibid., 26.

59. Ibid., 10.

60. Ibid., 36.

61. George Sayer, *Jack: A Life of C. S. Lewis* (Wheaton, IL: Crossway, 2005), 174.

62. Lewis, *A Grief Observed*, 9.

63. Ibid., xxv.

64. Ibid., 9.

65. Ibid., xxvi.

66. Han N. Baltussen, "A Grief Observed: Cicero on Remembering Tullia," *Mortality* 14, no. 4 (2019): 355. Baltussen recounts the archbishop's remark from A. N. Wilson, *C. S. Lewis: A Biography* (London: Collins, 1990), 286.

67. See Baltussen, "A Grief Observed," 355; and Wilson, *C. S. Lewis*, 285.

68. Wilson, *C. S. Lewis*, 285.

69. See Megan Devine, *It's OK That You're Not OK: Meeting Grief and Loss in a Culture That Doesn't Understand* (Boulder, CO: Sounds True, 2017), 20.

70. Megan Devine, "How Do You Help a Grieving Friend?" YouTube, July 18, 2018, https://www.youtube.com/watch?v=l2zLCCRT-nE.

71. Devine, *It's OK That You're Not OK*, 20.

72. Ibid., 24.

73. Lewis writes: "I almost prefer the moments of agony. These are at least clean and honest. But the bath of self-pity, the wallow, the loathsome sticky-sweet pleasure of indulging it—that disgusts me." Lewis, *A Grief Observed*, 6.

74. Wilson, *C. S. Lewis*, 286.

75. Elisabeth Kübler-Ross and David Kessler, *On Grief and Grieving: Finding the Meaning of Grief through the Five Stages of Loss* (New York: Scribner, 2005), 47.

76. Fred Rogers, *The World According to Mister Rogers: Important Things to Remember* (New York: Hyperion, 2003), 58.

77. See Jean-Charles Nault, OSB, *The Noonday Devil: Acedia, the Unnamed Evil of Our Times* (San Francisco: Ignatius Press, 2013). For an insider's point of view, as well as a masterful analysis of depression, read Andrew Solomon's *The Noonday Demon: An Atlas of Depression* (New York: Scribner, 2002). For Gloria Anzaldúa's most mature writings on her depression, see "Now Let Us Shift . . . Conocimiento . . . Inner Work, Public Acts," republished as chapter 6 of what was to be her dissertation, *Light in the Dark/Luz en lo Oscuro*, edited by AnaLouise Keating (Durham, NC: Duke University Press, 2015).

Chapter 4. Recoloring Depression

1. In 1990, one thousand disability rights activists protested outside the Capitol Building by attempting to climb up the stairs without wheelchairs, canes, or crutches. The "Capitol Crawl," as it is now known, resulted in the signing into law of the Americans with Disabilities Act by President George H. W. Bush. See Becky Little, "History Stories: When the 'Capitol Crawl' Dramatized the Need for Americans with Disabilities Act," History, July 24, 2020, https://www.history.com/news/americans-with-disabilities-act-1990-capitol-crawl (accessed March 16, 2022).

2. Andrew Solomon, "Anatomy of Melancholy," *New Yorker*, January 12, 1998, 44–61.

3. Andrew Solomon, "Depression, the Secret We Share," TEDxMet, October 2013, https://www.ted.com/talks/andrew_solomon_depression_the_secret_we_share?language=yi.

4. American Psychological Association, "Depression," https://www.apa.org/topics/depression (accessed February 28, 2022).

5. Solomon, "Depression, the Secret We Share."

6. Lou Marinoff, *Plato, Not Prozac! Applying Eternal Wisdom to Everyday Problems* (New York: HarperCollins, 1999).

7. Cara Murez, "1 in 3 College Freshmen Has Depression, Anxiety," *Health Day News*, December 6, 2021, https://www.usnews.com/news/health-news/articles/2021-12-06/1-in-3-college-freshmen-has-depression-anxiety (accessed February 28, 2022).

8. In 1966, a pharmaceutical company commissioned the Radio Corporation of America (RCA) to create the album *Symposium in Blues*, with songs from Louis Armstrong, Leadbelly, and Ethel Waters. The album was listed as a "promo," and the note reads: "A presentation album from Merck Sharp & Dohme. Includes a product insert for Elavil (amitriptyline)." See Gary Greenberg, *Manufacturing Depression: The Secret History of a Modern Disease* (New York: Simon & Schuster, 2010), 23; and *Symposium in Blues*, RCA, 1966, https://www.discogs.com/release/1630999-Various-Symposium-In-Blues.

9. Peter Kramer, *Against Depression* (New York: Viking Penguin, 2005).

10. Meaning "dark-skinned," *Prieta* was also a family nickname that Anzaldúa's mother used for her and that she used for herself in her writing.

11. Ann E. Reuman, "Coming into Play: An Interview with Gloria Anzaldúa," *MELUS* 25, no. 2 (2000): 31.

12. Gloria Anzaldúa, "On the Process of Writing *Borderlands/La Frontera*," in *The Gloria Anzaldúa Reader*, edited by AnaLouise Keating (Durham, NC: Duke University Press, 2009), 187.

13. Gloria Anzaldúa, "La Literatura: Contemporary Latino/Latina Writing," reading delivered at the Twenty-Fourth Annual UND Writer's Conference, March 24, 1993, University of North Dakota, https://commons.und.edu/writers-conference/1993/day2/3/.

14. Gloria Anzaldúa, *Interviews/Entrevistas*, edited by AnaLouise Keating (New York: Routledge, 2021), 78, 87, 93. See also Gloria Anzaldúa, "La Prieta," in *This Bridge Called My Back: Writings by Radical Women of Color* (New York: Kitchen Table/Women of Color Press, 1983), 199–201.

15. Anzaldúa, *Interviews/Entrevistas*, 169.

16. Anzaldúa, "La Prieta," 199.

17. Anzaldúa, *Interviews/Entrevistas*, 31.

18. Gloria Anzaldúa, *Light in the Dark/Luz en lo Oscuro*, edited by AnaLouise Keating (Durham, NC: Duke University Press, 2015), 174.

19. Anzaldúa, *Interviews/Entrevistas*, 93.

20. Anzaldúa, "La Prieta," 199.

21. Anzaldúa, *Interviews/Entrevistas*, 83–86.

22. Ibid., 86.

23. About her mother Anzaldúa adds: "Yet while she would try to correct my more aggressive moods, my mother was secretly proud of my 'waywardness.' (Something she will never admit.) Proud that I'd worked myself through school. Secretly proud of my paintings, of my writing, though all the while complaining because I made no money out of it." See Anzaldúa, *This Bridge Called My Back*, 201.

24. Anzaldúa, *Interviews/Entrevistas*, 85.

25. Ibid., 94. In another interview, Anzaldúa said: "I was called selfish. I was reading and writing. I wasn't doing housework, I wasn't helping. I wasn't socializing. I was selfish." Ibid., 227.

26. Gloria Anzaldúa, "Memoir—My Calling: Or Notes for 'How Prieta Came to Write,'" in *The Gloria Anzaldúa Reader*, edited by AnaLouise Keating (Durham, NC: Duke University Press, 2009), 235.

27. Søren Kierkegaard, *Søren Kierkegaard's Journals and Papers*, edited and translated by Howard V. Hong and Edna H. Hong (Bloomington: Indiana University Press, 1967), 5.556 entry 1793 (VIII.1 A 640); and Søren Kierkegaard, "Guilty/Not Guilty? A Story of Suffering an Imaginary Psychological Construction," in Søren Kierkegaard, *Stages on Life's Way* (Princeton, NJ: Princeton University Press, 1988), 188–89.

28. Gloria Anzaldúa, *This Bridge We Call Home: Radical Visions for Transformation*, edited by Gloria Anzaldúa and AnaLouise Keating (New York: Routledge, 2002), 551; Anzaldúa, *Interviews/Entrevistas*, 38.

29. Anzaldúa, *Interviews/Entrevistas*, 189.

30. Anzaldúa, *Light in the Dark/Luz en lo Oscuro*, 174.

31. Ibid., xvii.

32. "Now Let Us Shift" was due to the publisher in 2000. Anzaldúa started working on it in 1999 and finished it in 2001. "As co-editors," Keating says, "we were able to negotiate an extension from Routledge and make space for her longer essay." Anzaldúa, *Light in the Dark/Luz en lo Oscuro*, 199. Anzaldúa published her essay first in *This Bridge We Call Home* in 2002, and she also intended it for her dissertation. It was reprinted in *Light in the Dark/Luz en lo Oscuro* in 2015.

33. Anzaldúa, *The Gloria Anzaldúa Reader*, 3.

34. Anzaldúa, *Interviews/Entrevistas*, 249.

35. Ibid., 289.

36. Ibid.

37. Gloria Anzaldúa, "Healing Wounds," in *The Gloria Anzaldúa Reader*, edited by AnaLouise Keating (Durham, NC: Duke University Press, 2009), 249. Copyright 2009, The Gloria E. Anzaldúa Literary Trust and AnaLouise Keating. All rights reserved. Republished by permission of the copyright holder, and the publisher (www.dukeupress.edu).

38. Susan Cain, *Quiet: The Power of Introverts in a World That Can't Stop Talking* (New York: Crown, 2012).

39. Anzaldúa, "La Prieta," 209.

40. Gloria Anzaldúa, *Borderlands/La Frontera: The New Mestiza* (San Francisco: Aunt Lute Books, 2012), 60.

41. Gloria Anzaldúa, "Letter to Third World Women's Writers" in *This Bridge We Call Home: Radical Visions for Transformation*, edited by Gloria Anzaldúa and AnaLouise Keating (New York: Routledge, 2002), 166.

42. Anzaldúa, *Borderlands/La Frontera*, 71.

43. Ibid.

44. In her notes, Anzaldúa once compared Plato's cave to a closet, from which emerge queer individuals who have freed themselves from chains of silence. See Anzaldúa, G., date unknown, [Plato], Gloria Evangelina Anzaldúa Papers, box 227, folder 2, Benson Latin American Collection, University of Texas Libraries, Copyright © Gloria E. Anzaldúa. Reprinted by permission of The Gloria E. Anzaldúa Trust. All rights reserved.

45. Anzaldúa, *Borderlands/La Frontera*, 71.

46. See Jean-Charles Nault, OSB, *The Noonday Devil: Acedia, the Unnamed Evil of Our Times* (San Francisco: Ignatius Press, 2013), 22–55.

47. Anzaldúa, *Light in the Dark/Luz en lo Oscuro*, xxi.

48. "As day swallows itself," Anzaldúa writes, "la luna rises, rises, guiding me home—she is my third eye. Her light is my medicine." Ibid., 22.

49. Ibid., xxi.

50. Anzaldúa, *Borderlands/La Frontera*, 68.

51. Anzaldúa, *Interviews/Entrevistas*, 241.

52. Anzaldúa, *Borderlands/La Frontera*, 69.

53. Anzaldúa, *Light in the Dark/Luz en lo Oscuro*, 171–72.

54. Anzaldúa, *Borderlands/La Frontera*, 71.

55. Ibid.

56. Ibid., 67.

57. Ibid., 71.

58. Ibid., 68.

59. Plato, *Theatetus*, 150a.

60. Anzaldúa, *Borderlands/La Frontera*, 71.

61. Anzaldúa, *Interviews/Entrevistas*, 225.

62. Anzaldúa, *Light in the Dark/Luz en lo Oscuro*, 111.

63. Anzaldúa, *Borderlands/La Frontera*, 71

64. Anzaldúa, *Light in the Dark/Luz en lo Oscuro*, 122–23.

65. Ibid., 119.

66. Anzaldúa, *Interviews/Entrevistas*, 248.

67. AnaLouise Keating, "Editor's Introduction," in Gloria Anzaldúa, *Light in the Dark/Luz en lo Oscuro*, edited by AnaLouise Keating (Durham, NC: Duke University Press, 2015), xxi.

68. Anzaldúa, *Borderlands/La Frontera*, 60.

69. Anzaldúa, *Light in the Dark/Luz en lo Oscuro*, 91.

70. Solomon, *Noonday Demon*, 365.

71. "In order to make any kind of change," Anzaldúa wrote, "you have to be in this kind of conflicted space. You can't get better at anything unless you have gone through the conflict. You have to be really shaken out of your customary space." Anzaldúa, *Light in the Dark/Luz en lo Oscuro*, 153.

72. Ibid., 91.

73. In 2002, Anzaldúa wrote about plans to get acupuncture and therapy, but each session cost $80 to $105, and she was already seeing "too many doctors." Ibid., 173.

74. Ibid., 172.

75. Ibid.

76. Ibid.

77. Jerome Wakefield and Allan V. Horwitz, *The Loss of Sadness: How Psychiatry Transformed Normal Sorrow into Depressive Disorder* (Oxford: Oxford University Press, 2007), 12–14.

78. Dena M. Bravata, Sharon A. Watts, Autumn L. Keefer, et al., "Prevalence, Predictors, and Treatment of Impostor Syndrome: A Systematic Review," *Journal of General Internal Medicine* 35, no. 4 (April 2020): 1252–75.

79. *Susto* is a Dante-like trip to the underworld—Mictlan—and it requires coming face to face with Coatlicue. Anzaldúa writes: "Behind the ice mask I see my own eyes. They will not look at me. *Miro que estoy encabronada, miro la Resistencia*—resistance to knowing, to letting go, to that Deep ocean where once I dived into death. I am afraid of drowning. Resistance to sex, intimate touching, opening myself to the alien other where I am out of control, not on patrol. . . . It ends with a thousand foot drop." Anzaldúa, *Borderlands/La Frontera*, 70.

80. "Andrew Solomon: The Stories of Who We Are," transcript of interview with Kate Bowler, *Everything Happens* (podcast), July 30, 2019, https://katebowler.com /podcasts/andrew-solomon-the-stories-of-who-we-are/.

Chapter 5. Learning to Be Anxious

1. Emily Tate, "Anxiety on the Rise," *Inside Higher Ed*, March 29, 2017, https:// www.insidehighered.com/news/2017/03/29/anxiety-and-depression-are-primary -concerns-students-seeking-counseling-services.

2. One study shows that, "among affected adolescents, 50% of disorders had their onset by age 6 for anxiety disorders." See Katja Beesdo, Susanne Knappe, and Daniel S. Pine, "Anxiety and Anxiety Disorders in Children and Adolescents: Developmental Issues and Implications for DSM-V," *Psychiatric Clinics of North America* 32 no. 3 (2009): 483–524. https://doi.org/10.1016/j.psc.2009.06.002.

3. The psychiatrist Marc-Antoine Crocq points out that today's focus on mindfulness likewise echoes what the Stoics preached. See Crocq, "A History of Anxiety: From Hippocrates to DSM," *Dialogues of Clinical Neuroscience* 17, no. 3 (2015): 320. DOI: 10.31887/DCNS.2015.17.3/macrocq.

4. Arlin Cuncic, "Therapy for Anxiety Disorders," VeryWellMind, June 30, 2020, https://www.verywellmind.com/anxiety-therapy-4692759.

5. One study showed that "even after treatment with CBT, up to 50% of children remain symptomatic, and many still meet diagnostic criteria." See Eli R. Lebowitz, Carla Marin, Alyssa Martino, Yaara Shimshoni, and Wendy K. Silverman, "Parent-Based Treatment as Efficacious as Cognitive-Behavioral Therapy for Childhood Anxiety: A Randomized Noninferiority Study of Supportive Parenting for Anxious Childhood Emotions," *Journal of American Academic Child Adolescent Psychiatry* 59, no. 3 (March 2020): 362–72, doi: 10.1016/j.jaac.2019.02.014.

6. For example, Patricia Pearson writes: "There was no awareness of anxiety as a category of illness—as opposed to the normal state of affairs—prior to the rise of office-based psychiatry in the twentieth century." Pearson, *A Brief History of Anxiety . . . Yours and Mine* (New York: Bloomsbury USA, 2008), 4; see also Crocq, "A History of Anxiety," 320.

7. Crocq, "A History of Anxiety," 320.

8. Ibid.

9. Christopher Gill, "Philosophical Psychological Therapy: Did It Have Any Impact on Medical Practice?," in Chiara Thumiger and Peter N. Singer, *Mental Illness in Ancient Medicine: From Celsus to Paul of Aegina* (Boston: Brill, 2018), 370.

10. Sigmund Freud, *The Question of Lay Analysis* (New York: Brentano, 1926) 62, 63.

11. David A. Clark and Aaron T. Beck, *Cognitive Therapy of Anxiety Disorders* (New York: Guilford Press, 2010), 11.

12. See Joseph E. Davis, "Let's Avoid Talk of 'Chemical Imbalance': It's People in Distress," *Aeon*, July 14, 2020, https://psyche.co/ideas/lets-avoid-talk-of-chemical-imbalance-its-people-in-distress; and Ashok Malla, Ridha Jooper, and Amparo Garcia, "'Mental Illness Is Like Any Other Medical Illness': A Critical Examination of the Statement and Its Impact on Patient Care and Society," *Journal of Psychiatry and Neuroscience* 40, no. 3 (2015): 147–50, doi:10.1503/jpn.150099.

13. American Psychiatric Association, "What Are Anxiety Disorders," https://www
.psychiatry.org/patients-families/anxiety-disorders/what-are-anxiety-disorders.

14. Cuncic, "Therapy for Anxiety Disorders."

15. Hayden Shelby, "Therapy Is Great, but I Still Need Medication," *Slate*, November 1, 2017, https://slate.com/technology/2017/11/cognitive-behavioral-therapy
-doesnt-fix-everything-for-everyone.html.

16. The psychologist Sheryl Paul argues in her 2019 book *The Wisdom of Anxiety* that even the most severe cases of anxiety are still not disordered. Sheryl Paul, *The Wisdom of Anxiety* (Boulder, CO: Sounds True, 2019).

17. Kierkegaard, *Journals and Papers*, 5.158 entry 5480 (letters, no. 21, n.d.).

18. Ibid., 5.232 entry 5662 (IV B 141, n.d., 1843).

19. "Five of Kierkegaard's brothers and sisters had died between 1819 and 1834. The two older sisters died at the ages of thirty-three and thirty-four. Kierkegaard's father thought that none of his children would live beyond the thirty-fourth year." See ibid., 1.511, note 164.

20. Ibid., 6.17 (IX A 99, n.d., 1848).

21. Søren Kierkegaard, *Practice in Christianity*, edited and translated by Howard V. Hong and Edna H. Hong (Princeton, NJ: Princeton University Press, 1992), 174–75.

22. Ibid.

23. Kierkegaard, *Journals and Papers*, 6.72 (IX A 411, n.d., 1848).

24. Ibid.

25. Ibid., 5.180 (III A 172, n.d., 1841).

26. For the Kierkegaardians out there, I base this claim on the fact that much of what he writes in *The Concept of Anxiety* is taken from his journals. This pseudonym seems closer to the real Kierkegaard than some of his others.

27. Ed Yong, "Meet the Woman without Fear," *Discover*, December 16, 2010, https://www.discovermagazine.com/mind/meet-the-woman-without-fear.

28. Kierkegaard, *Journals and Papers*, 1.39 entry 97 (V B 53:23, n.d., 1844).

29. Ibid.

30. Kierkegaard, *The Concept of Anxiety*, 45.

31. Maria Russo, "9 Books to Help Calm an Anxious Toddler," *New York Times*, January 18, 2020, https://www.nytimes.com/2020/01/18/books/childrens-books
-anxiety.html.

32. I'm reminded here of Chimamanda Adichie's concept of the "single story." In a single story, anxiety is terrible. But in a complex story like Kierkegaard's, it's also thrilling and can be productive. See Chimamanda Adichie, "The Danger of a Single Story," TEDGlobal, July 2009, https://www.ted.com/talks/chimamanda_ngozi
_adichie_the_danger_of_a_single_story?language=en.

33. Kierkegaard, *The Concept of Anxiety*, 44–45.

34. Ibid., 44.

35. Ibid., 45.

36. Ibid., 61.

37. Ibid.; Gordon Marino, *The Existentialist's Survival Guide: How to Live Authentically in an Inauthentic Age* (San Francisco: HarperOne, 2018), 44.

38. Kierkegaard talks of being "educated" by anxiety. Kierkegaard, *The Concept of Anxiety*, 121; see also Rollo May, *The Meaning of Anxiety* (New York: Washington Square Press, 1977), 341.

39. Kierkegaard, *The Concept of Anxiety*, 121.

40. Anzaldúa, *Borderlands/La Frontera*, 60.

41. Kierkegaard writes: "The object of anxiety is a nothing." Kierkegaard, *The Concept of Anxiety*, 77.

42. See Arlin Cuncic, "6 Tips to Change Negative Thinking," VeryWellMind, June 29, 2020, https://www.verywellmind.com/how-to-change-negative-thinking -3024843; and Arlin Cuncic, "Overcome Negative Thinking When You Have Social Anxiety Disorder," VeryWellMind, April 30, 2021, https://www.verywellmind.com /how-to-stop-thinking-negatively-3024830.

43. Irving Yalom, *Staring at the Sun: Overcoming the Terror of Death* (San Francisco: Jossey Bass, 2009), 201.

44. Ibid., 117.

45. Anzaldúa, *Borderlands/La Frontera*, 60.

46. Glennon Doyle, *Untamed* (New York: Dial Press, 2020), 50.

47. Glennon Doyle, *Carry on, Warrior: The Power of Embracing Your Messy, Beautiful Life* (New York: Scribner, 2014), 28.

48. Doyle, *Untamed*, 89.

49. Kierkegaard, *Journals and Papers*, 5.258 entry 5743 (V A 71, n.d., 1843).

50. Ibid., 2.360 entry 1919 (X5 A 44, n.d., 1852).

51. Marino, *The Existentialist's Survival Guide*, 53; Kierkegaard, *The Concept of Anxiety*, 155.

52. Yalom, *Staring at the Sun*, 277.

53. See Paul, *The Wisdom of Anxiety*.

Conclusion. Practicing Night Vision

1. Lorde, "The Uses of Anger," 127.

2. Anzaldúa, *Borderlands/La Frontera*, 101; Henry David Thoreau, "Walking," in *The Portable Thoreau*, edited by Jeffrey S. Cramer (New York: Penguin, 2012), 402.

index